T0206775

The
Book
of Joe

The Book of Joe

About a Dog and His Man

Vincent Price

Vincent Price (signature)

Illustrated by Leo Hershfield

With a New Preface and Introduction

Copyright © 1961 by Vincent Price

Preface copyright © 2016 by Victoria Price

Introduction copyright © 2011 by Bill Hader

Cover design by Mauricio Díaz

978-1-5040-3040-3

This edition published in 2016 by Open Road Integrated Media, Inc.
180 Maiden Lane
New York, NY 10038
www.openroadmedia.com

To the memory of my mother and father whose love for pets and people gave purpose to their lives and their children's.

Preface

Children are like anthropologists. They gather clues about life by observing the world around them. And the thing children most want to learn about is, of course, love.

As the child of a man who was adored by everyone he knew or met—family, friends, and strangers—numbering into the millions, a man who loved many people, places, and things (art being his greatest and most public passion), learning about love from my father was tantamount to being taught how to swim by being tossed into the Pacific halfway to Hawaii and being told to head for shore. Whatever he did, he did it *big* and with his whole heart. Love was no exception. So I just swam in the sea of his love and let the currents take me.

But ultimately, when it comes right down to it, children are pragmatists. While I could feel my father's huge heart in everything he did and every encounter I witnessed, I realize now that I learned the most about how to love by watching my dad with his dogs. What I learned was that when love is true, it is simple, sweet, and shared.

Dog is Love.

That would be my three-word synopsis for this wonderful little book—my favorite of my father's books. I am not the first person to believe that dogs crack open our hearts in ways that other human beings sometimes can't, just by being totally present and loving unconditionally, no matter what. In doing so, they help us to be better people.

Joe found my dad at a time of great upheaval, during a nasty divorce that took his son away, followed by the deaths of both his parents. To say my father loved Joe makes the word "love" suddenly seem inadequate—as words often are to describe the feeling of giving your whole heart to someone. But in the end, it is my father's words, his gift as a storyteller, that allow us a glimpse of the sweet, simple, shared love between a man and his dog.

Vincent and Victoria Price with Puffie the pug
From the personal collection of Victoria Price.

I was very young when Joe passed. There would be many more dogs in our lives: Paisley the Skye Terrier, Puffie the pug, Pretty the Pekingese. (All P's—you'll find out why when you read this book!) My stepmother brought her Chihuahua, Tiggy (short for Antigone), with her from England when she moved to California. More Chihuahuas followed: Maile and Fendi. The last dogs in my dad's life were two Schipperke sisters, Willi and Kiki. My dad loved them all in the darling uncomplicated way we dog lovers love our dogs. But Joe was special—as you will read in this love letter from a man to his dog.

Vincent Price with his last two dogs, Willi and Kiki

From the personal collection of Victoria Price.

This gem of a book has been out of print for a very, very long time. It gives me great pleasure to reintroduce readers to one of the sweetest love stories I have ever read, written by a man who taught me as much about love as anyone I have known. World: Meet Joe, the four-legged love of Vincent Price's life!

Victoria Price
Lifelong Dog Lover
Santa Fe, New Mexico

Introduction

The first time I saw Vincent Price was in a Tilex commercial. I was six years old and the experience was pretty traumatic. But my mom calmed my nerves, saying, "That's Vincent Price. He always plays scary people but in reality he's a very nice man. He's just pretending." In reality? What do you mean? I just saw him in a chamber of horrors scrubbing mildew off a shower wall. Are you saying that's not his house? That's not his shower? And the hunchback guy isn't his roommate?

Not too long after this, I was up late watching TV and caught *House of Wax*. At first I was scared—it's the guy from the Tilex commercial!—but I remembered my mom's words: He's a nice man, he's just pretending. I relaxed and by the end was completely enthralled.

As I watched more of his films I realized that I was receiving my first lessons in acting: Be committed and have fun. That was the constant in every Price performance. And it's what kept bringing me back again and again to his movies. By the time I was in high school I was a fanatic. One of my first purchases with my lawn mowing money was a box set of six of his Edgar Allan Poe movies. I had a *Tomb of Ligeia* poster in my room. I was a card-carrying Vincent Price geek.

Years later, not long after I'd been hired as a cast member on *Saturday Night Live*, a writer on the show, Matt Murray, suggested we try out a Vincent Price sketch. I'd been doing my Vincent Price voice in the office (really just ripping off Dana Gould's impression) and it was making us laugh. What if he had a series of holiday specials in the late '50s that were always being ruined by the stars of the day? We did the first one for Thanksgiving and it went great! It was a real moment for me. I'd just played my hero on my favorite show!

I love it when teenagers tell me that the Vincent Price sketches inspired them to check out his movies. It's the least I could do for the man who taught me the basics.

It's a true honor to be a part of this book.

Bill Hader

The
Book
of Joe

Chapter One

This is a tale of how I went to the dogs or, to be numerically correct, to the *dog*. Now please do not expect this book to end with a glorious proclamation of rehabilitation. Not a chance. After fourteen years I'm incurably hooked on, intoxicated by, and addicted to—my dog, Joe.

No candidate for a show ring, my Joe. The only kind of ring with which he's familiar is the one he inadvertently but unremovably dyed in the dining-room rug. Dear but tactless friends have remarked that Joe is ugly. They make sport of his hairy, pointed ears; his legs that bow before and waddle after; the sweep of his tail (so luxurious even I have to admit it's slightly ridiculous . . . kind of like a waif wearing mink); they consider his color untidy and his nose tough as a truffle. Well, either they're blind or I am, because the older he gets the stronger these debatable charms take their claim of me.

As I'm writing this, he is comfortably curled up on my feet. That is, he used to be able to curl when he was slimmer. Now his position at my feet could probably best be described as *lumped,* and the sound accompanying this lump these days—a muted symphony of snorts and wheezes—is not unpleasant save, perhaps, that it harbingers the winter of his existence, a thought that causes a lump in my throat . . . and one I'll happily forgo for now.

Through fourteen years of togetherness, with life's inevitable highs and lows, there have been times when Joe has offered me more humanity than humans could. Between Joe and me there is only one line of communication: affection. And it is the only communication system I know of that so seldom needs repairs. Attention, vigilance, yes. But the power that feeds it has the soul as its source—the basic dynamo that makes us all go—and I go all the way with Joe.

I'm a man who needs a lot of definitions. I have a library that, by no means totally definitive on any subject, does somewhat placate my inquisitiveness about the whys and hows of lots of things with lots of answers. On the subject of man's relationship with dogs, however, I can find little explicit information. There are volumes on how this relationship affects men, and a few attempts to tell how it affects dogs—not, unfortunately, firsthand from a dog. But apparently the fact that it does exist and has existed since the beginning of time is taken so for granted that no author I can find has felt called upon to try to explain why. There it is. Most men patently love dogs, and dogs, for the most part, apparently love men.

So much whimsey, sentiment, and bathos have been

written about it that one is almost put off attempting it once again, especially one determined to avoid some of the above approaches. The whole subject seems somehow to sum itself up in a somewhat saccharine statement that a man's best friend is his dog. This devastating declaration, which quite blandly eliminates the possibility of man's liking his own kind anywhere near as well, no one seems concerned about. And every day, now that I'm hypersensitive to it as a statement of fact, I see new evidence of its truth.

For example, there's the brute who belts his wife in the jaw, dresses his children down with a stream of toothsome oaths, then turns to his pet and purrs it an earful of sweet talk that would put a traveling salesman to shame. He will order his family around like a sergeant, and then wait, hand and foot, on his four-pawed friend, whose watery eyes will only reproach him for his kindness by demanding more. No effort is too great to make his animal feel as a man's best friend should: beloved. To hell with the wife and kids.

At a gala party one night, in the best of company, suddenly two poodles arrived, unannounced, and immediately took over all conversation, social intercourse, and two of the far-too-few chairs. Exquisite ladies in fashionable creations and priceless jewels put the fragile seams of their dresses to unendurable stress in inelegant positions to get on a level of social exchange with the poodles. The men, usually voraciously hungry and thirsty at the cocktail hour, became abstaining circus trainers in their efforts to lure the poodles away from the ladies with fancy hors d'oeuvres and even the martinis. The host and hostess turned into an ogre and ogress who gave evidence of wishing that we'd all go home so they could enjoy their dogs by themselves. For the half hour of the poodles' stage center not a single sentence was exchanged by the guests unless by someone who, made unbearably homesick for his own dog, frantically tried to divert attention from the poodles present by relating laborious tales of the cute intelligence and acid acumen of his own Scotty, beagle, Dalmatian, basset hound, or—pardon the expression—poodle—with a much fancier clip and better disposition.

One guest who quite obviously prided himself on his rugged masculinity went completely limp and lisped a long sentence of baby talk to one of the dogs and, catching himself at it, quickly directed his attention toward somebody else's wife, but so self-consciously and quickly that a touch of unbecoming baby talk remained in his hot pursuit of her charms.

My search and research for a clue on the subject of this strange behavior has brought me no definitive answer. However, the proverbs of all nations, as well as the vernacular, are filled with homely references to dogs, such as the old American saw that defines man's three good friends as "An old wife, a dog, and money." There's little question in my mind that this is an admirable trinity. Of course, it could be modernized with other adjectives: "A *young* wife, an *old* dog, and *much* money."

"After a time, even a dog makes a compromise with a cat." So say the Hungarians, contributors to female felininity in the persons of some of the most glamorous ladies of stage, screen, and boudoir. Perhaps one of this same type of lady, some time back, invented another Hungarian proverb: "Dogs bark, money speaks."

"Going to the dogs" is always a phrase applied to people who are easing out of life's responsibilities and having a helluva good time doing it. But just so we won't hurt the feelings of our canine friends, once the slider hits bottom, we never say, "He's made it! He's at the 'dogs.'" And can it not be said that in "going to the dogs" the trip may often have been started by a "hair of the dog that bit you"?

Suffice it to say that man's literature is full of references to dogs, and I only regret that dogs have no literature to be full of men.

There's another familiar adage: "Every dog has his day." Well, Joe and most dogs I've known have not only *their* day but most of mine and parts of other people's, too. When the day isn't theirs, you'd better get them to the vet's. They're sick.

So, back to the "day" of Joe, which, as I've mentioned, began fourteen years ago.

It was the eve of Christmas Eve. Clouds were low with the promise of rain. California's answer to a white Christmas is, more often than not, a wet one. But rain in the Sunshine State can bring with it all of the coziness of snow, if you let yourself dream a little. If you're an actor, between "assignments" you have a drink and make toasted cheese sandwiches. At least I do. And if it's Christmas time, you set about all the happy chores of that happy season, which you never expect to be sad.

But on this occasion Christmas loomed a couple of days ahead, like the funeral of hope. By mutual agreement my wife and I had parted. She took our five-year-old son and went to stay with friends, and Christmas walked out with my boy, leaving me unseasonably and unreasonably desolate. No . . . not unreasonably. I love Christmas. I had come from a happy home and Christmas was the happiest of family times. Perhaps my parents had their problems too, even at Christmas, but if they did they kept them well hidden, and whatever might have been showing was blurred to my eager eyes, peering at the miracle of Christmas from behind rose-colored glasses.

Throughout our lives, no matter what our ages, most of us anticipate the holidays. We look forward to their happiest fulfillment. We never really expect a *bad* Christmas. But that sad eve of Christmas Eve, I looked forward to only one thing: having it over with. It seemed that the whole world was sinking around me and I was alone, a monument to loneliness, beneath those canyon sycamores laden with mistletoe, with only misery tall enough to reach my height and kiss me.

All I had were the dogs. An empty house and the dogs—one, a brindle bitch who, mongreled some generations back, still looked like what might have been an early ancestor of the Norwegian elkhound. She had been named "Golden Blackie" by my son because of her black-tipped, golden fur. The other, her pup, Panda, also named by my boy because he was a woolly black and white ball of fur, was the only one we had kept out of a litter of twelve, sired by a disagreeable but ever-lovin' mutated brute who lived up the street. By this Christmas, Panda was a happy, prancing, almost-mature puppy dog, as black as black coffee, except for an immaculate white chest dickey. His greatest pride was an ebony plume of a tail, behind which Sally Rand would have been proud to hide her ample charms . . . if possible.

I was mighty grateful for the dogs and took them with me as I did some feeble, last-minute shopping. At home they were close at foot as I wrapped half a heartful of gifts for my boy and threw up some disconsolate decorations around the house. They sensed my desolation at the whole procedure and gave what loyal animals always give at such a time—an added sense of despair—as they dragged behind every move I made, and, whenever and wherever I lit, made two heaps of furry dejection at my feet.

I trimmed a tree in the knowledge that the boy would spend some little promised time with me on Christmas Day. I even hung up a stocking—but lower this year—for I felt that Panda, in his present mood, wouldn't have enough spunk to think of it as his own, as he'd done the year before, when he was a voracious, bent-pawed ball of a pup. The year before, Panda had eaten the stocking and its contents, leaving for hungry Santa's visit only a forlorn, half-chewed tangerine.

Panda had lost his pep. I was right. Once the stocking was in place and within his reach, he simply put his heavy chin on the curb of the fireplace and eyed it sadly, while Goldie consolingly bathed his face with her currycomb tongue.

By noon on Christmas Eve, a little blurred on beer, I went sound asleep on the floor in front of the unlit fire. The last thing I remember was that Goldie had decided that I needed a bath too, and was starting gently with my ear.

When you live in a narrow California canyon, there are two sounds that strike terror in you: a siren . . . and screeching brakes. They announce the two possibilities of disaster: fire or—because there are no sidewalks—an accident in which someone or something has been hit, or almost.

Screech! Silence . . . ! And I was awake and off the floor and out the door and in the street. A woman ran toward me, mumbling how sorry she was. What about? My dog.

There, on the neighbor's lawn, lay Goldie, whimpering and licking her leg. It was broken.

Somewhere out of the leftover terror of being awakened by that screech—out of my beer-bruised brain—out of the burden of that new aloneness—came the longest continuous line of curse words I've ever mustered up in my life. This careless carful of people had hurt my dog and I damned them with every word of hate I'd ever heard until their car slunk down the canyon with its spare between its wheels and disappeared. Then I called our good vet, who appeared almost before I hung up. He gave Goldie a quieting shot, bound her leg, and took her off to the hospital, leaving me with the assurance that she'd be all right in a week or two.

I called the friends with whom my wife was staying and told them to tell her about Goldie. I hung up, had a real drink this time—whiskey—and quickly I was completely awake and as sober as a member of A.A. in good standing.

It was time to feed Panda and eat something myself, then wait out Christmas Eve or, if I were lucky, sleep it out. I whistled for that big black mutt. I needed him and, with Goldie gone, he'd need me.

He didn't come.

I've always found that dogs are much more sensitive than we give them credit for being, especially when we think that something isn't going to affect them. And, in the same light, they can drive you crazy with insensitivity when you think that they've had a tough time of it, by not caring a hoot in hell for your concern for them.

I was afraid that Panda might have tried to follow the vet, or have gone off up the street in complete indifference to Goldie's plight. Either way, I had to find him, so I searched the house and then the garden.

Up on the back terrace, sticking out from under a pitisporum bush, bent with its Christmas splendor of red berries, I spied his large black plume of a tail. I snuck up on it and gave it a gentle yank. No wag. I lifted a berry branch and there was the rest of him, quiet as he'd never been . . . dead.

He'd been hit and had taken off on the impulse that he was still alive, only to die a hundred yards away, under the bush with the Christmas-red berries.

I buried him near the bush, and then I sat down on the ground and cried—for about an hour. My God, how it hurts a man to cry! Not from masculinity abused or from vanity or fear that someone will see you. It just plain hurts. This time it hurt so much I didn't even think of doing what I always had done the few times I'd cried before: look at myself in a mirror. This was a sadness I didn't want to see and certainly didn't want to remember.

"Merry Christmas!" The first jerk who said that to me was going to get the most un-Christian cold shoulder ever given for free!

I slept the Eve away, waking every once-in-the-night with the cold anticipation of having to tell my boy that his dogs were hurt, and that his special, loving one was dead. And yet I slept late in the subconscious knowledge that there would be no early tugging out of bed to open stockings this Christmas morning.

Little boys are enchanting creatures. They are merrier and more inconsequential than little girls. Little girls learn so soon what they are, and to play it for all it's worth. Little boys aren't on the make for anyone. I had dreamed, ever since I was one myself, that someday I'd have one—a boy child. This boy was my dream come true. Blond, loving, sensitive, and completely boy. My profession had kept me away from him enough that my responsibility to him weighed pretty heavily. But now I would have to live without him, with only the usual "normal visiting rights," every-other-weekends in which to try to be a father; odd holidays to make desperate passes at his affection. And here was the first of these, the togetherness of his family still day-fresh in his mind; bewildered by why he was not in his own room; why he and his mother were away from home at Christmas . . . and where was I?

The few hours he would be with me, this greatest of all children's days, we wouldn't have a chance to repair any of the present or future punctures in our relationship, or even patch up this immediate hole in our Christmas stocking. Goldie's leg was broken, Panda was dead, and I had to tell him that the only things still entrusted to me of our old security were hurt and beyond hurt.

Had it been my fault? Hardly, since the dogs were always allowed to run free. But I indulged myself in a shallow wallow of self-recrimination and decided that it was no escape. The facts existed. I had to face them.

My son was coming in the door any minute and I had to make the best of it. Some crazy notion made me run up to the back terrace, fashion a crude cross of red berries, and put it on Panda's grave. What I expected that to mean or do I had no idea, but it made me feel better and I'd pretty much decided that anything that would make me feel better was the thing to do. Misery loves self-indulgence.

He arrived, full of love and of tears that came like a quick little storm, soothing but violent while it lasted, for the sun was not far away. In our joy at seeing one another the tears stopped, at least long enough to let us open the presents, and they would make him forget to cry—I hoped.

Our hours were eaten up with Christmas fun and we parted with mutual promises that everything was going to be all right and that I'd call him tomorrow.

He was gone . . . and all at once I realized . . . he'd never mentioned the dogs, and I had psychosomatically forgotten to tell him. Merry Christmas! It was over.

The day after Christmas should have a name too, as Christmas Eve does. It should be equally anticipated and often is, I'm sure. That year, 1947, it had a name for me like the end of a prayer . . . Amen!

Chapter Two

It was the day after Christmas, 1947. So be it.

Pico Boulevard, which runs the length or breadth of Los Angeles—I never know which it is—has never really "made it." Main artery though it is, drawing the tired blood off downtown Los Angeles, its lively moments are mornings when the blood pours into that empty heart, and late afternoons when the congestion is let. Halfhearted businesses line its curbs, but many seem to lose heart altogether, for they aren't there next time you look for them. One shop, however, thrives and proves, perhaps, that Los Angeles has a heart, after all. It's a pet shop, devoted to the unpedigreed of all species. Cocky little lovebirds of impure color; pigeons who neither pout nor fan their tails; kittens, cute in a card of colors from orange to black, but mostly variegated, and pups whose family trees make Burbank's experiments with grafting look like unadulterated corn. The clientele is legion, for who can resist an animal unburdened with chic? And the day after Christmas, 1947, was no exception. The legion was lined up to take these waifs from the limbo of obscure ancestry to the highest echelons of a guaranteed happy home.

I was sixth in line, but I could have been twenty-sixth, so great was my determination to get back on the horse of happiness, which had so violently thrown me two days before. I wanted another dog because I'd almost never been without one, except for a short cat period, since I was a little boy.

I knew that Goldie, when her leg had mended, would no longer be my charge, belonging as she did to my boy. She would live, perforce, where he lived. And I felt deeply that if my house were to keep any identity as a home, even a part time home, for my son, a dog tag would give me at least some license to his affections. It could just be that I wouldn't be identity enough. Anyway, I wanted a dog for my own needs as well as his and ours.

That the dog was man's first domesticated animal is pretty well determined now by whatever kind of "ologist" it is who does that sort of thing. Maybe it boils down to the simple fact that we like what likes us. I, for one, have always been a little suspicious of those die-hards who won't leave well enough alone and try to make pets of cobras, tigers, or turkeys. Anyway, the mutual best-friend pact between dogs and men is good enough for me. I like dogs and, especially, I like mutts.

I love the fact that mutts can only be called dogs. They aren't poodles, Pomeranians, or Pekingese. They don't claim Afghanistan or Scotland, Norway or France as the home of their breed. They can, and do, come from everywhere, and no matter what accident of birth may make them favor one specie over another, regardless of temperament or physiognomy, they still look and act like mutts. Essentially they act like dogs who know that they are dogs and are happy with their role in life, not like dogs that think they are people and give me a terrible sense of inferiority.

If I were a dog, I'd like to be a mutt, and, come to think of it, as a person I prefer being a mutt too, not too closely identified with any race, which I'm not, being English, Welsh, French, and heaven knows what else. As a matter of fact, it's what I like about being an American. We have all the best mutt characteristics until we become grand or take ourselves too seriously.

But to get back to sixth place at the pet shop. The lady ahead of me was poking a tobacco-stained finger into a cage of lovebirds who fluttered screechingly to the opposite side and resumed their beak-combing of each other's feathers. Linesman Number One was in the throes of indecision over a splay-legged kitten or a nosy little hamster. Both looked equally miserable, held up for inspection in his two big hands. The hamster won and left with its new family in a cardboard carton. Much giggling went on as the two children in tow vied for preference as to who would sleep with it the first night, and who the second—if it survived.

Number Two settled for a vicious, semi-feathered parakeet whose plight as the picked-on one had won her sympathies. I suspected that her new pet was the real heavy in the cage, and probably deserved all the peckings he had so obviously received. Lovebirds, indeed . . . But you could be sure that if she got him every feather would be fostered back with loving care. The lady candidly fancied herself as having a way with our feathered friends. Her conversation with the owner was testimony to triumphs of tenacity in the matter of how to win birds and, one wondered, how to lose influence with people.

Number Three voiced definite disappointment that there were no monkeys, though no one knew how he expected nature or the store owner to achieve a mixed-breed monkey. But apparently he was not about to consider any other animal or bird or fish, so he left empty-handed. Perhaps he was one of those commercial voyeurs who like to be in on what other people buy and always want what isn't available . . . or is already sold.

It was getting close to me, and while I knew what I wanted, I was so fascinated by the other purchasers and purchases, I wasn't looking at the stock. Number Four brought me to my senses, however, as he held up for his daughter's inspection the cutest white-eye-patched, lop-eared nothing of a puppy dog I'd almost ever seen. My heart did a little jealous turn and then went all out to White-Eye, whomsoever's best friend he ended up. And, of course, who could resist him? The little girl, snuggling him close enough for him to get in a couple of deal-clinching licks on her nose, pleaded with Papa who immediately succumbed and put me in second place . . . but with a slight sense of defeat, having missed a chance to take home Lop-Ear, the surest way to a child's heart . . . and I desperately needed one.

The lady with yellow fingers just ahead of me, now being Number One, took full advantage of her position and proved to be one of the greatest animal shoppers I have ever seen. What she would have done to a big-game safari in Africa! Before taking a shot she'd have examined each animal from head to hoof, making sure that it was a worthy quarry. There was the reassuring thought that, in Africa, some one animal might not have stood still for her categorizing of its physical virtues or faults and would have eaten her—or at least ripped her to bloody shreds. But these poor little waifs in the Pico Pet Farm had no comeback and had to submit to all kinds of indignities, only to be discarded like contaminated rags when they met with her disapproval.

I hoped, for one glorious moment, that they would all be spared having her as a mistress, platonically speaking, of course, but she was not the type to go away empty-handed. I began to concentrate on the possibility of her choosing a particularly yappy, parti-colored, miniature poodle, since there were no boa constrictors on the menagerie list, and, by cracky, it worked. She paid her money and took her choice— the little loudmouthed polka-dotted poodle. As she carried it out, having refused to buy a small cage or accept the gift of a cardboard carton, it leaped out of her arms and scooted off down the street. I felt silent prayers go up from all of us left in line that it would get away. But the speed with which she set out after it left no doubt who would be the loser in its last mad dash for freedom. Two minutes later she thrust a triumphant head in the shop door and announced that the tiny prodigal was safely locked in her car. But poodles are pretty clever, and I, for one, hoped for the possibility that it had started the car and driven off without her.

Now there I was, confronted with one of man's most terrible decisions: the selection of a pet. Being momentarily alone in the world, I was spared that terrible indecision that happens between man and wife in these affairs. And since I had had the wit not to plan for my boy to be in on it, I didn't have to look forward to the adorably disturbing statement from him that all the puppies were cute, so why not take them all home with us?

I guess that puppies know when someone who has a

great desire to adopt one of them for life is near. At least all of these seemed to sense my desire to own one of them, for they put on the greatest show of salesmanship I've ever seen. Each one played an individual role, and they all displayed their bags of tricks by whining, barking, scratching the wire of the cages, lying on their backs, pink bellies up, or hiding their unpedigreed, captivatingly winsome little faces between their dappled paws. But I was not about to be had by any of this nonsense. Anyone who was going to be my best friend for the span of his lifetime had to be more than cute and less than demanding. He had to have the essential dignity of a mutt, with just enough charm and not too much temperament.

All these profound requirements went through my mind, even though I knew that I hadn't a chance of achieving any of them if one of these little beasts took it into its head really to win me.

It must have been my very real need for the right pet that finally made me look deeper into one of the cages of attention-seeking-and-getting mongrels, for back there, looking like a miniature Trafalgar Square lion, lay Joe. I knew instantly that this was my dog and that his name was Joe, and something in his look at me said: "Master, Friend, Pal . . . Hello! I'm Joe."

He didn't give me the full thrust of his charm . . . just a steady thrash of his tail. It was a tail in full plume, exactly the color of a tortoise-shell cat. In fact, all of Joe was covered with silky, orangish-brownish-blackish fur, except for his paws and chest, which were lily-of-the-valley white.

This, then, was Joe. Dog of dogs. Short-legged, slightly bowed in the front and splay-foot behind, curl-tailed, with ears like a flying fox and a face that, if there are dog angels (and I'm sure there are), was an angel dog's face. His expression was just sad enough to convey his pity for mankind and wise enough to make you wonder if he wasn't right to pity us.

When I told the salesman that it was Joe I wanted, he told me, semi-disgustedly, that he had been marked down from five dollars to three fifty. I never knew that they had bargains on angels, but when they do, you'd best take the advantage.

While he was making change from the five-dollar bill I gave him (Joe's original price), he told me the virtues of the other pups in the same cage, all of whom were Joe's brothers and sisters. They were so much cuter, according to him, more lively, better marked—he didn't dare say better bred—and, according to him, I was making the greatest mistake of my life.

Apparently, Joe was the mistake, and I was making him mine!

I told him that it was a mistake I was willing to pay for now, and, I hoped, for many years to come. If our conversation had continued, it might have risen to great philosophic heights. But it ended with the return of the dollar fifty I had saved on Joe and the handing over of Joe himself.

The rest of his family bid him a noisy farewell when Joe was fetched from the rear of the cage, where he sedately remained. He merely yawned a wide-mouthed, curl-tongued yawn and waited for all the nonsense to be over. Joe knew, and I knew, the secret of the ages . . . that a man and his dog don't need to be sold to each other, and that no one and nothing can unsell them once the bargain is struck.

The salesman must have had some secret confidence in my choice, for, instead of offering me a cardboard box or trying to sell me a carrying cage, he tied a piece of clothes-line around Joe's neck and gave me the other end. And after Joe had shaken himself free of the dust of the cage and his boisterous family, we marched out of the shop and into the world of man and dog.

Dignity is innate. Man or dog, you either have it or you don't. Joe had it. We walked down the street to the car, he at a discreet distance ahead to make the way safe for me. Then suddenly he stopped to do what little dogs do when they have to, and, as though in apology for not being old enough to know how he should do it, he gave me an over-shoulder look that assured me it wouldn't be long till things were dog-shape. Then, standing once more, he shook himself from nose to tail tip so violently he fell over on his back. Once upright again, another look told me not to worry . . . that he was still little and that dogs mature quicker than men do and, though this might happen several more times, he'd get his land legs and, from then on, he'd keep his feet firmly on the ground and his eyes on me.

Chapter Three

Joe came into my life at an empty moment and he did much to make that moment short, for there's nothing quite so fascinating and time-consuming as watching a pup grow up. Like most men, I can't wait for children to grow up—mine and other people's. Babies scare me half to death with their fragility and, even when they're a little older, with their inborn wisdom and determination to do what they want to do. Then, just before they become people, there is a period when, no matter what you do, they make you look silly doing it—an abstract idea I needn't elaborate on to any father.

But pups should be, and are, forgiven anything during these few helpless months before the world of instinct has taught them all the tricks and they settle down to a dog's life of studied receptivity of human attention.

Joe was an adorable puppy. Even his most consistent detractors had to admit that. He was pert, affectionate, and ferociously alive. But because he had no obligation to any one breed of dog, he immediately abandoned the nonsense that full-bred animals sometimes carry to a point of boredom and became what he is—a dog. He learned his household manners early and resorted to minor misdemeanors only to express his indignation at a reprimand for being especially doglike, or at being left alone too long without attentions of food or love.

The deafening silence of my house was broken by Joe's presence, and the loneliness alleviated considerably. Of course, he was no replacement for lost loves. Rather, a new entity . . . beautifully equipped to steer attention away from myself and my sadness of the moment.

My boy adored this new four-legged homemate, and Joe dutifully permitted the haulings, yankings, and gentle tuggings of a five-year-old without so much as a yip or a nip. The boy's visiting days were full of squeals and fun, thanks to my dear furry friend, and when they were over, Joe would collapse on his little back, all four feet pointed ceiling-ward.

He had one youthful folly that almost amounted to delinquency: the carrying off of shoes. But two or three of them, thrown violently in his direction, with one a direct hit, and he was cured to the point where a shoe became, in his maturity, a symbol of adoration and an object of security. To this day, while members of his family swim at the beach or in the pool, Joe stands station by their shoes. Occasionally, if the swim takes too long, he may add a drop or two of his own identifying odor to compliment theirs. But then, I'm the only one who's ever caught him doing this, and it has remained among the many precious secrets that we share.

Early in the game we developed little signals of affection that flag our individual and separate needs for love. When he does the familiar front-paws-out and hind-end-up obeisance to me, I gently crush his toes with my foot. I love to kiss his silk-soft snout, and he, just to keep me guessing over the depth of his affection, inevitably takes this as a cue to sneeze so violently he sometimes hits his leathery nose on the floor with a loud thump. But then, to reassure me that he liked the kiss (and, I suspect, the sneeze), he rubs the length of himself against my trouser leg as a gesture that, while completely as reassuring as he meant it to be, is a little disconcerting when you find that you're wearing cowboy chaps of questionable-quality fur.

One posture of love imposed on dogs—that of being carried in human arms—while charming with a tiny dog, is something to which larger types never adapt themselves gracefully. Much as they may want to accept the indignity of this position, the look on their faces is a dead giveaway that life would go on much more happily if you'd just put them down where they belong . . . on all fours. True as I know this to be, there were, and are, moments of frivolously expansive love for Joe that make me have to baby him, and the look of suppressed horror on his face when he sees this coming rates high in my cherished pictures of him. He can never quite make up his mind what to do with his legs. They stick up, helter-skelter, into the air, helplessly ill at ease but resigned to abject discomfort. He tolerates this position with a look of coy foolishness and, since he's learned that I can keep a straight face just as long as he allows it, when I put him down in a fit of delighted laughter, he shakes his shaggy coat back into its accustomed disarray and gives me another look, this time saying: "Well, Dad, had your fun, haven't you? Thanks for making me look a fool."

As he grew up, Joe became a beloved feature of the canyon. He grew fat on the favors of many of its inhabitants.

Still, he was able to keep what little shape he had to begin with by the enormous amount of exercise he indulged in daily. He walked miles to visit human friends for tidbits, and canine ones for company and other things, inspecting trees for new scents, and old scents to keep his sense of direction. He possessed that remarkable gastronomical timepiece that all good freewheeling house dogs boast and that brings them home at food time no matter how far afield they might have gone during the day.

After he had been struck off the list of shoe eaters, he took up the fetching habit of retrieving empty cans and cartons from the incinerator and garbage pail and walking blindly with them clenched in his jaw, covering his snout, to secret places where he would bury them in graves shallow enough to allow some of their succulence to invite him back for further sniffing. Half of my work as gardener was digging these treasures out of the flower beds, since even the indomitable force of nature has a hard time piercing a tin can. My bulbs took a heavy beating, rooted out of the ground at all stages of growth. But heavy or light beatings couldn't take Joe's mind off the pleasures of this pursuit.

I even tried the classic cure of tying a cottage-cheese carton (one of his favorite quarries) around his neck, but the look of dejection as he hobbled around the yard was too much to bear, and, of course, if the same hand removes the punishment that imposes it, the point is lost.

Whenever or wherever I drove, up or down the canyon,

I would come across Joe, his tail sweeping the wind like a dainty duster. He was always in the gutter, as there were no sidewalks, and, as you watched him, he'd disappear up a driveway or between hedges, seeking some attention, or setting about to give attention to some detail of his daily routine. In our youth together I would occasionally open the car window and shout a cheering greeting at him. But the almost imperceptible pause this caused in his peregrinations soon taught me that our relationship was still strictly domestic and that Joe preferred it to being confined to the house. This suited me fine, with one drawback: even now he rarely comes when you really want him unless it suits his mood and fancy.

The independence of his character is best illustrated by one of the most surprising events that ever happened to me. About a half mile down our canyon, toward town, stood some charming houses that, for one reason or another, changed occupants frequently. One in particular had been tenanted by three different friends of mine, all actors. But each time I thought the possibility of having actor neighbors was faintly pleasant they moved away.

Shortly after I remarried, Barry Sullivan and his wife bought the much-tenanted house, and, since Mary and I liked them both, this seemed a very desirable thing. But, not being given to rushing into neighborly relationships quickly, we let six months or more go by before we got around to asking them to dinner.

During cocktails that evening the swinging door opened surreptitiously and Joe oozed into the room. I was about to ooze him out, when Mrs. Sullivan gasped: "Brownie! What are you doing here?"

Who the hell was Brownie?

It turned out to be Joe. *My* Joe. What came to horrible light was this: Joe spent all day, every day, at their house. They had a female puppy and he had attended her growing up with big-uncle affection. Then, when she was a girl, he proceeded to bestow upon her the blessing of eight little Joes. After the birth of the octuplets, never a day went by that Joe wasn't there, playing with his babies. As far as the Sullivans were concerned, he was their dog, though they admitted to being mystified about his nighttime and early-morning activities. But the regularity of his day-time visits and his apparent adoration of his family made them overlook this idiosyncrasy, and he was duly named Brownie and adopted into the Sullivan family.

After we revealed the fact that Joe was our dog, general good humor prevailed and we toasted Joe, their female mutt, his spouse, and all eight Price-Sullivans. Things were pretty wet out that night, but it certainly cemented our friendship. This friendship was further reinforced some months later when Joe sired another eight puppies. All sixteen of Joe's children found happy homes, so no strain was put on our new-found, neighborly relationship. But there is hardly an area in or around Beverly Hills where Joe-type dogs may not be found, meandering independently up and down the canyons and streets.

The instinct to re-create his image is stronger in Joe than in most dogs. Perhaps for this reason, and his enormous success in satisfying this instinct, he has none of those embarrassing frustrations that less sexually articulate ones feel and that induce in them the necessity to give other than polite attentions to elderly ladies or, even worse, to men who don't know what to do about it but giggle and try to divert the unwanted attention elsewhere.

Love is not a fleeting matter for Joe. He puts his heart and soul in it . . . and like all good lovers he likes to take his time. He has a disturbing, even terrifying habit of going A.W.O.L. for three to five days when the love bug bites, and, though by now I know the cause of absence, a panic comes upon me about the third day that sends me haunting the hills, the pound, and even that ghastly place where they take dead animals, to find him. Each time, he eventually returns, pounds lighter, sheepishly prodigal, and once more I realize that the beast in man is not nearly so well scheduled or disciplined as the beast in beast.

Joe is elderly now and, being somewhere around fourteen years old, if you can believe all those old wives' statistics about one year of a dog's life being equal to seven years of human life, he's really ninety-eight. But if this is true, he's a mighty lusty ninety-eight.

His last memorable romance took place a few months ago

and happened thus. Next door to us, in our present home, lives a charming elderly couple whose children are all grown up and gone. They mind their garden and their own business with perfect neighborly decorum, and our acquaintanceship with them is that all-American ideal of non-gossipy chitchat over leaf-raking and hedge-trimming. They have infrequent visits from well-mannered grandchildren who know our name and use it with Mister and Missus in front of it—the few times we meet over a lost ball from their yard or a lost dog from ours. The only permanent resident member of the family is an elderly, mammoth gray and white English sheep dog named, unimaginatively, Moppet.

Moppet's history is a saddish one of a boy's pet left behind by a call to war. After the war a "Dear Moppet" letter arrived, announcing a human love in foreign parts, and Moppet, because of her size and age, could hardly become the perfect partner in a design for living in a newlywed apartment, so she was left behind.

I don't think Moppet could have cared less. The grandparents were kind to her; she had her yard and, as age crept on, an increasingly small run of the neighborhood. Her occasional visits away from home were finally whittled down to slow, shaggy visitations on our front steps. Moppet, matted and blinded by her floppy forelocks, could still find her way up our long front stairs to throw herself like a shag rug in front of our door. Her aged detachment and perfume made it impossible to get close to her, and so my family boiled their efforts down to a gentle "Hello, Moppet," and an unspoken avoidance of patting her usually dirty head.

Her unruly appearance was really not the fault of her involuntary owners. They tried to keep her brushed, but she loved to soothe her aged skin by rolling in the oil drippings on various driveways and then powdering it down by further rolls in mud and dust. As her neighbors, we assured ourselves that beneath her eccentrically unkempt exterior there probably beat a heart of gold. But in our own dogs there was gold enough to satisfy all affections, so we left this Sierra Madre source unexplored.

But apparently not Joe. I had never seen him give her more than a sniff, in passing . . . but Moppet had a season left in the old girl and, like Darby and Joan, one day they went off into the hills to croak a last duet in the best tradition of Nelson Eddy and Jeanette MacDonald: "Smilin' through the Years."

Four days of frantic searching it cost me before my neighbor dropped by to see if we'd seen Moppet. Then I knew what was up and settled back to await Joe's exhausted and embarrassed return.

Joe returned and recuperated in a few days and was his old bouncing self. Moppet, alas, love-spent and lorn, died a few weeks later, but, as the old saying goes: "What a wonderful way to die."

Chapter Four

Joe has a tremendous sense of responsibility to his people, especially if they are sick. I've had a lot of dogs in my life, but I've never known one with such built-in sympathy for human misery. Perhaps he feels akin to the no-kin-all-kin inheritance of most of us in America.

Usually it's the other way around. People make fools of themselves over sick animals, but Joe makes a fool of you because he has much more dignity where the physical condition of man is concerned. It's almost as if he felt that he could take some of your illness into himself, so adhesive is his attention. Nothing can unloose him once he decides to poultice himself to a sick friend until the aggravation is gone, even though Joe may end up the main aggravator, as the following should illustrate.

Mary and I were involved in a student fancy-dress ball for the benefit of an art organization of which I was the president. My position made it necessary for us to go all out in our effort, if not to be the most lavishly costumed, at least to be the most imaginatively. So we commissioned an artist friend to design something for us that we could execute ourselves and that would put us ahead of our time as a "space couple." The outcome was long underwear, dyed black, with black stocking caps that fitted like helmets, down into the neck. We were black from head to toe, with black masks over our eyes and, on top of our heads, a triple-tiered set of strobo-lite plastic propellers, the kind that kids run with against the wind at amusement parks.

The ball was a ball. We felt that we were spectacularly stylish and everything went well until someone offered me a cigarette: I couldn't carry any in my long underwear. I took it and then had a hell of a time trying to light it, as I couldn't yet take off my mask. I couldn't connect the match with the cigarette, so, fumbling around with one match after another, suddenly the whole book went up. I had had to hold it so close, trying to see what I was doing, that when the flare-up happened, it went off in my right eye. The pain was short and intense, but it didn't seem to be serious, and in the general merriment I forgot about it and went on with the party.

Two days later I was in agony. My eye couldn't tolerate any light, so I sat in the darkest room in the house with a waterfall trickling down my cheek and a steady mumble of protestations pouring out of my mouth . . . and Joe directly under my feet. I tripped over him on the way to the kitchen, fell over him as I staggered to get deeper into the dark, kicked him, and unintentionally stepped on his paws and tail a dozen times, but nothing could discourage either his constancy or his position underfoot. Joe had become my seeing-eye dog, but, not having the etiquette or training of that magnificent corps of human helpers, he almost caused one disaster after another as I jumped over him, fell over him, bumped into him, and finally picked him up bodily to put him outside, out of my harm's way.

But once outside, he stood by the door, howling, or scratched on it until he was let in to take up his perilous vigil at, and on, my feet.

When night came, the pain would let up a bit and Joe could be talked into lying a foot or so away. But that was all. A sudden groan from me and he was back, closer than ever.

This kept up for some five or six days, in spite of Mary's devoted nursing and expert ocular treatments, and Joe, I suppose, did take time to see to his supper and other natural duties, but when I don't know, for it seemed that we were one . . . a clumsy one, and sixlegged . . . one strange creature, half man, half beast, inseparable, and only vaguely ambulatory.

Whenever I was able to take my mind off my own troubles, with my good eye I would contemplate Joe, and the pain behind his eyes as he looked up at me in sympathy was infinitely worse than the pain in mine. Joe's theory is that misery loves company, but who is more miserable I'll never know, until one day Joe tells me— which, undoubtedly, he will.

But his concern for people in pain was not just for me. It was catholic. I was not the only one to be soothed by his affection. His humanity—for it is human, or perhaps it's only our conceit that makes us think that we have a corner on the caring market, the thinking heart, the feeling mind—but his caninity, let's say, goes out to all . . . master, mistress, fellow-dog and fellow-friend.

Like everyone from a devoutly family home, I have a dozen "relatives" by heart, people my family loved so much they became "cousins," "aunts," and "uncles." My mother was especially given to padding the family tree with these mistletoe relatives. Not that they were parasites, as mistletoe is, but in the other sense of that berried greenery, they were "kissing cousins." All of ours were functional as friends, and all were fun to be with. Their periodic visits in our home were as much (if not more) anticipated and enjoyed than those of some of our blood relatives. They claimed only our friendship, which is a much more tolerant claim than the stake of blood.

One of these, who was my mother's maid of honor at her wedding, had double dominion in our family because she had made herself a second daughter to my mother's mother, whom we all adored. Our grandmother was an independent beauty who lived her own life, welcome to lean on us each year long enough to save something of her tiny income so that she could get off on her own again. On her own she spent a great deal of time with this foster daughter of hers, whom we called Cousin Georgia. The two of them shared many an adventure and were "modern" women in the best sense of the word, long before modernity settled into being an unquestionable virtue in the gentle sex. They were truly gentlewomen; elegant, independent, excited by life—their own and others'.

Cousin Georgia had always had to work for a living. She had been widowed early in her married life and had no family of her own—parents or children. She used what little money she'd been left to travel, see the world, and try to find a place in it for herself. The few times she came to visit us, or we went to visit her, were wonderfully inspirational to me. She loved the theater, the arts, all those staples that a lady alone can stock her mind with to make wherever home happens to be a palace of delight. I delighted in her company and, after my grandmother died, I became her seldom-seen but devoted child. Then, when my mother died, we took on an added relationship, and, living as we did in the same city, I tried to share a little of my life with her. There were no demands either way . . . just gratitude on both sides that we had inherited each other.

She was a game, grand dame, this ersatz cousin of mine. During World War II she went to the university and took a course in metallurgy, hoping to be of some use in the war effort. Later on she lied about her age and, looking the lie because of her vitality, she had a steady job in one of the big department stores in Los Angeles. Holidays were our times together, to which she always brought thoughtful gifts and wonderful treats. She had a multitude of friends and, since the necessities of her life were very small, her friends and her family—mine—shared her largesse.

She was a great lady whose pluck made her vital because it was part of her, not something put-on. She didn't have to keep a stiff upper lip. She came from that generation born with it, plus a straight back and a flexible mind that made living something to do just because you were alive. But even this generation of snipers at boredom couldn't altogether handle one man in their lives: Old Father Time.

One Thanksgiving Day, while driving her home from dinner, I noticed a wistful resignation in her usually profuse thanks for sharing the holiday with her. Although she was not the kind of lady you could question about herself—because she knew all the answers, for herself at least—this wistfulness could be interpreted as an invitation to probe a little. Anyway, I felt that I had to take it as such, and I probed.

The story that came to light was so dear, so sad, so devoid of self-pity I could hardly keep from crying. She started by telling me something she'd never even told my mother or grandmother—that her husband had committed suicide. It was some financial failure or other, so many years before that, in the conviction that money should never take a life, even she had forgotten just what it was. It just wasn't worth it. She had determinedly taken what was hers and decided to make it live for her. So, after some wonderful and enriching trips all over the world, she started her widowhood with nothing. She was perfectly capable and willing to support herself and she had, her whole life. She confessed to the lie about her age, and to a small concern that someone in the department store would find out. She had to admit that, after all, a woman at seventy-eight might have a hard time getting another job.

Seventy-eight! I was thirty-eight and worried about my future! She wasn't really so worried about hers as she was about being found out in that little lie. I wondered if she was really only seventy-eight.

Then, briefly, she told me of her only relative, a brother who was eighty-three and a recluse, living in the hills of Arkansas, and then, quite casually, she said: "You know, I've always wondered how I was going to die. Now I know. My doctor told me last week that I have cancer. That's not a bad way to go, for someone my age. But there are so many things I'd still like to do. I'd like to live a while in Carmel, for instance. I'd like to see Egypt again . . . but that's too far, isn't it?"

I wish that I could have sent her, then and there, to Egypt, but I couldn't. However, I offered to send her to Carmel and she turned me down.

"I have a little saved and I can get there if I want to go. But I'm afraid to go, because I want to live there . . . I don't want to die there . . . Well, good-by, my dear, and thank you once again."

I drove away with a lump of elation in my throat. What a lady . . . And a prayer in my mind: "Dear God, let me be like that, if I live that long."

Cousin Georgia did go to Carmel. She lived there three months. She did let me help a little, but one day I got a secondhand message from a friend that she wanted to visit me. I knew at once this meant that she wanted to die near me, and so I sent her the fare and she took her first plane ride down from Carmel and came to "live" with us.

Joe was about a year and a half old when Cousin Georgia came to die. She lived three months and, from the moment she set foot in our house until they carried her out, he never left her side. We worried, because he insisted on sleeping in her room, that he might upset her, but she sensed his love and his sensitivity and wanted him there.

The day she died, Joe watched her to the hearse, then trotted off down the canyon and didn't come home for four long days and nights. The pain she had borne and he had tried to share went slowly out of him as he unacquainted himself with death, and when he came back, it was life as usual, full of its small adventures and large loves, with and for the living.

Chapter Five

From the time Mary and I were married and Joe found himself with a "mother," their relationship has been one of the joyous banes of my existence. Mary is as much a dog lover as I am, but to her a dog should have a pedigree, or, if it doesn't have a pedigree, it should be some recognizable kind of a dog. Joe is recognizable only as a dog, as I've said before. It's even difficult to say that he's part this and part that, so perfectly is his ancestry blended. Any special breed that may be traveling in his genes is strictly incognito. He has a coat of many colors, paws of another, and the only thing you can say about his facial features is that they're canine. Some breeds look like wolves, sheep, etc., but Joe looks like a dog, definitely.

Mary was never allowed in her youth to have a dog. Her father was a landscape architect with an excusable professional aversion to dogs, and besides they moved from place to place around the globe, as the British will, and a dog was a domestic impossibility, I guess. Anyway, she never had one.

When we met, she had cats. She is much more tolerant of racial mutations in catdom than in the kingdom of dogs. Her cats, one of which was named for me, were cats. Independent brutes they were, the three of them, whose nomadic spirits fitted in perfectly with her bachelor-girl way of life. If she was gone for the day at work, a can of cat food, opened in the morning, sufficed for their moody appetites, as they saw fit to appease it whenever and however much. Cats are like that.

Come to think of it, Joe has a great many cat traits, and perhaps that's what confused Mary when she became his stepmother. She expected him to behave like a dog, to be more regular in his habits, and to stay at home, when and if wanted or needed. But I had always let him have his head. He was allowed to come and go as he wanted and, actually, he was pretty regular in his goings-out and comings-in, except at times of sexual duress, when he could hardly be held accountable—the air being full of fragrances too hot for any red-blooded dog to handle with equanimity. Besides, his musical protestations, if freedom was denied him at such times, definitely had to be turned off in the interests of neighborhood sleep. Joe in love is hi-fi and stereophonic.

I don't believe that Mary is any different from other women who move into a man's life. It is their nature to rearrange it, to put it nicely, or bluntly . . . to change it completely. She changed mine, I must admit, for better or worse who will ever know? Certainly not I, because I love her and we all know that love is, if not blind, blindfolded.

But if Joe has any traceable origins, while not visible, temperamentally there's something of the bulldog in him. The bulldog comes from England, and so does Mary. It's been a ten-year tug-of-war between the two, and, up to now, even the Marquis of Queensberry, while abhorring the tactics used on both sides, would have to call it a draw.

They are evenly matched, histrionically, temperamentally, endurance-wise, and, though the battle they wage is all-out war, the ambushes and sallies, direct advances and retreats, the diplomacy used in inviting allies to one side or the other, the subterfuges and ruses, delays and prognostications make it one of the most fascinating tactical maneuvers to watch in the history of modern cold warfare.

I am the innocent battleground on which this war is waged, and it wouldn't surprise me to see poppies sprout out over the acreage of my body when, one day, I'm retired like Flanders Field by the victory of one party or the other. Though I fear it's a war to the death . . . perhaps mine!

Since Joe already had an unequivocal ally in me and a mercenary in my houseman, Will, Mary inherited, through marriage, a small enemy army she was perfectly capable of conquering singlehanded. She must have felt that it would be a lonely victory, so during the first year of our marriage she sought recruits in the form of goldfish, parakeets, and a cat named, generously, Josephine.

The goldfish really were no competition to Joe. He scorned their existence by lapping most of the water out of their bowls or ponds, leaving them on several occasions gasping and flopping in little of their natural element. The parakeets he ignored except when they escaped, and then he assumed the best traits of some of his possible ancestors, stalking them straight-tailed and back-bristling, moving stealthily toward his quarry. When he came too close, they screeched and abruptly shattered his pose and poise into a helter-skelter, rapid retreat, tail between the legs. In the frustration of not knowing how to carry out his bird-dog assignment, he sought the protection of the kitchen and surer food.

A dear friend gave us a small green parrot, whom we named after him, Charles A. Greene. We were told that he was semi-trained, that with a little patience and love he could become an adorable pet who would sit on our shoulders and eat out of our mouths. Repulsive as both of these prospects were to me, I tried to help Mary, who relished the idea, to carry out the course of training. With more love than patience on my part, Charles did learn to sit on my shoulder and, with a wary eye on him always, I could slide from room to room, proving nothing except myself some kind of imbecile. But Mary doted on the picture and there are many candid shots of me, looking like a gargantuan St. Christopher with that ridiculous little bird nibbling on my ear or just sitting there with a much wiser look on its face than there is on mine.

In a terrible moment of whimsey I thought that it would be fun to teach Charles to ride Joe around the house. Charles was delighted by the whole idea, but not Joe, who flew out from under him on wings of fright and wasn't to be found near the training ground for days to come. But Joe's a sport, and the day did come when Mary was able to get another photo of the most abjectly miserable dog in the world, mounted by a triumphantly cocky green parrot. The look on Joe's face was too much for me, and I put my foot down on further degradations like this. Charles made many overtures toward rides on Joe, but I stood by my guns and one day grabbed Charles just as he was about to sneak up on Joe while he was napping . . . and for my pains received the full clench of his powerful beak on my finger. Charles flew away, with the help of my painful propulsion, to sulk for some hours on the top of the bookcase. Two days later he was traded in at the pet shop for a cockatiel whose vicious nature made it imperative to keep him caged—much to the delight of both man and dog.

We had noticed that, unlike most dogs, Joe had no particular aversion to cats. He rarely chased them, and once we even saw him go after another dog who was about to tree a big tom. A friend had offered us a kitten who was the cat image of Joe. Mary, who sees herself as a sort of Jane Addams of the animal world, was all for accepting it then and there, but I persuaded her not to talk it over with Joe, which would have been the humane thing to do, but to talk it over with me, which was wiser. And besides, she was surer of getting her way with me.

I have a deep conviction that men are born losers in marital arguments, and have ample proof that I'm right. One of the greatest proofs was the advent of Josephine in our lives.

Josephine was adorable. She and Joe looked like unidentical twins, trying to look alike by wearing the same fur coats. I don't know what made us assume that she was a girl, because she had the disposition of a prize fighter. She shadow-boxed Joe's tail, his nose, his ears, and he accepted it all with fatherly forbearance. He almost seemed to like it, and every once in a while we'd find Josephine firmly squashed under his paws, languishing in the most luxurious shampoo from his long tongue.

While Joe may not have had the same questions concerning her sex that we did, I actually don't think that he had any questions about her species, either. He treated her as another dog . . . and a puppy. So Josephine perhaps became one of the first puppy-cats in history, for she too didn't seem to worry about what Joe was. He was her delightful companion, pussy-dog Joe.

The short happy life of Joe and Josephine ended mysteriously. They were inseparable, and since Joe could hardly be expected to become a house dog after the freedom of his upbringing, we were forced to the conclusion that she followed him too far afield one day and perhaps ran afoul of less cat-loving dogs, or one of those indiscriminate cat killers, the automobile. We searched the canyon but never found her, and while it upset us a great deal and set Mary back a long way in her quest for a pet of her own—and an ally against a

Joe-dominated home—he, on the other hand, couldn't have cared less. A dog of the world must accept these things, and Joe continued to reign supreme in the not too peaceful kingdom of our home.

I think that Mary was utterly tolerant of Joe up through the episodes with the goldfish and the birds, and she came closer to a real fondness for him than ever before when he took to Josephine with such unquestioning *savoir-faire*. But Josephine's disappearance was, in some way, connected with Joe's habits of cruising the canyon, and, although Mary could not blame him directly for it, she never quite forgave him for leading her pet to a fate that was probably no worse than death. Nothing I could say in his defense seemed to console her for Josephine's loss, and so when another friend (will they never learn!) offered us the prospects of a poodle puppy from a projected litter, I had to go along with the suggestion that another little stranger come into our lives, like it or not.

The fact that the friend's lady poodle had not been bred yet didn't deter Mary. She tackled the problem like the expert color consultant she is and spent days going into the bitch's background and that of prospective studs to see if she couldn't (with their help) achieve a white one.

The lady in question was gray, and the stud, carefully studied and finally selected, was brown. But my Mendelian Mary had found enough white genes lurking in their pasts to assure a white male, according to her calculations. When Mary makes these summations (or in this case consummations) in that abacus brain of hers, I don't question. I've learned that, sooner or later, the laws of chance will prove her right. Or it could be that her blind faith in her own theories of proven theories is guided divinely by a power that doesn't want to see her proven wrong. It would be too embarrassing for it, and too difficult to explain to her.

Be that as it may, the result of this particular plan produced an Oxford-gray female . . . one Oxford-gray female, and that's all there was to the litter. No blacks, no browns, no whites . . . one gray bitch.

I was in hopes that this ultimatum of nature would make our donor so suspicious of Mary's divine right to be a dog breeder he would want to keep the heiress himself. But Mary was way ahead of me and convinced him that the Great Dog Father had so ordained events because, more than anything, she wanted an Oxford-gray female poodle who, in turn, would produce a white male—or several white males—that she would then return to him as proof that this was only the first step in the inevitable evolution of the greatest breed of white poodles ever seen.

In due course, a ball of Oxford-gray fur entered our lives and again, in due course, completely took them over.

Prudence, whom I suspect Mary named because of her prudent planning for the future of the breed, was an irresistible puppy. All puppies are, but Prudence couldn't be resisted because she wouldn't be. She played the role of only girl child right to the hilt, copping attention from all the other flora and fauna in our menagerie household, including Joe, and even people began to count less and less as her poodle personality became more and more pronounced.

The floors of our house were stone and, while she had a few rugs to keep her well-padded behind from being chilled by it, she had to sit on every piece of furniture, including us. When the trying period of training her out of this habit was in process and she was being gently but firmly swept onto the freezing floor by loving, determined hands, she would show utter contempt for the reprimand by seating her hindquarters sedately on Joe.

My love for Joe is so full of these memories I may seem to go beyond the limits of love to maudlin sentimentality. But believe me, if you could recall as I do the picture of Joe—his big, flat brown head and black snout like patience off its monument . . . completely swamped by this fluffy ball of gray-black fur—even you might throw discretion to the wind and cry with hysterical joy that such a dog exists. And, in that he's mine, such extravagance may be excusable.

Mary will never excuse it! To her, Joe should have been proud to be Prudence's pedestal, and perhaps he was, for to this day he doesn't seem to mind being sat upon. I feel that I can learn a lot from the dignity with which Joe suffers the slings and arrows of such outrageous fortune. The earth is the footstool of the Lord, and Joe is of the earth—earthy—and minds not being the footstool of man or beast, though he prefers beast.

But, love Joe as I do, I must admit that Prudence has her points. Unfortunately, they are not the points a poodle is meant to have to be a prize poodle. Mary slipped up somewhere, because Prudence's ears are too short and her nose is too long, and her front legs, being shorter than the rear, give her a look of always being about to come in for a landing. She is rather a girl hockey player when it comes to being feminine, but she is sweet. She exhibits such a terrible case of the cutes when called by name it belies her girl-guide attitude of "Tennis, anyone?" at the drop of a bone. Her dog-dish manners are deplorable, since hunger is her constant companion, and only on the threat of obey or starve will she take tidbits politely. If you make the mistake of holding out on her too long, you're liable to slide the full length of the room in a puddle of drool.

To pay Joe back for comforting her in her infancy, she now bathes his graying face with a foot-long tongue and sometimes coaxes him into a friendly tussle in which the two of them, baring savage tusks, pretend that they're hyenas, snapping and gurgling in a seeming duel to the death.

When Prudence had won the first heat in her race to womanhood, Mary began to do research for a mate to cool the second.

One day I was taken to a very chic interior decorator's shoppe, run by two personable young men, on the pretext that their East Indian brass and copperware might be suitable for the Turkish corner Mary had been planning in our Spanish-type house. Logical? Of course. In fact, I was beginning to enjoy a mental picture of myself, sitting cross-legged on a hassock, smoking hashish, when I was brought back to reality by the prancing of a huge, white, boy poodle as he made sniffing overtures to his old friend, Sneaky Mary. She called him by name and I called myself a couple, having been taken in like an idiot. Bulls in china shops, yes. But poodles in decorators' shoppes? . . . Especially the kind with two *"p's!"*

As Mary posted the marriage banns with the two young men, I sent a telepathic message to Joe: "Here we go again, buddy!"

Prudence submitted herself to the ordeal with alacrity and, some time later, presented us with eleven puppies. The one thing she hadn't inherited from her mother was singleness of purpose, or, perhaps like many only children, she determined to have a big family. Either way, she had them, and for all the fears I had that Mary would never be able to part with any of the pups, however many there should be, I reveled with Mary in the miracle of their birth and even more in the miraculous instinct with which Prudence, who had led a sheltered life till now, attended their birth and immediate after-birth cares.

There were, as I said, eleven puppies. Two didn't survive, but the other nine were full of life, blindly pink-toothed, nuzzling their mother for food. We were both so enchanted with this undulating pen of hungry beasts we really didn't notice, until two days later, that all of them were gray or black. Not one white. Prudence's genes predominated, and I wondered if perhaps the decorator daddies of her husband hadn't succumbed to the temptation of having him bleached to go with the white décor of their shoppe.

Mary was crestfallen, though brave, but the eternal mother instinct took over completely as she cuddled and cooed over each little brute in turn. The more in love with them she became, the more worried I got. What in heaven's name do you do with nine standard-sized poodles, plus Prudence . . . plus Joe . . . etcetera.

Naturally, any idea of giving them away before they

reached independent puppyhood was out of the question, so whatever fears I had about keeping them all had to be allayed for at least eight weeks by my own fascination with their extraordinary individuality, almost from birth.

Since the advent of Prudence all animals in our house have had to have names beginning with "P"—our name being Price. A new parakeet, for instance, was named Pocahontas; a skunk we caught in the garbage can, and toyed with the idea of domesticating, was named Phew. And so the search for such names was on in earnest when the nine pups appeared.

Prudence's pups were named Paderewski, Pinto, Pansy, Patience, Penelope, Picayune, Percival, Pablo, and Pasquale . . . and poor Joe! Just so he wouldn't feel left out he was nicknamed PJoe!

PJoe was undaunted by these new boarders in our kennel. As a matter of fact, he took to them as if they were his own. After all, his parental instinct was highly developed, having sired sixteen that we knew of. He visited Prudence's family when they were little, with her approval, walking among them with gingerly steps and occasionally setting a helplessly overturned one aright so that it could wiggle over to mother for refreshments.

As they grew up and Prudence's inborn sense of discipline made them mind their manners, around her at least, they took to Joe as a tolerant uncle who made them think that he never tired of playing with them. When they were old enough to be allowed carefully overseen visits into the house, they followed their mother's example of avoiding the cold stone floors by sitting on him. One day I caught four of them suspiciously huddled in a corner. I thought it to be a sort of gang attempt to break training, only to find, underneath the heap, old Uncle PJoe, a living carpet, languidly accepting this newest deprecation of his dignity.

Only one of the nine, Picayune, had even the remotest possibility of being a good poodle. She had no white; the others were all parti-colored with the most adorable white collars and cuffs or white dickeys, or, in one instance, a lopsided white patch over one eye, matched on the other side by a white ear.

To Mary these mismarkings were signs that the white supremacy of our variegated poodle breed was coming to the surface, so she chose Picayune to be the mother of future white generations and the one for us to keep out of the litter.

The monster of the nine was named Pasquale. He was the most forward at food time and always got there first, both at Prudence while she was nursing them, and later at the huge bowl of mush. He invariably got the most until the others discovered that, by crowding in on him, they could crowd him out. Many a time I would find him sitting dejectedly on the side lines, howling or whimpering, until I put him back in the bread line.

The result of this little tragedy was that Pasquale got bigger and bigger and more and more dependent on human help, and, of course, had I only been bright enough to realize it all the time, he was worming his way into my affections . . . consciously, I'm sure. When the time came to find the pups new homes, it was sentimental old Dad who couldn't stand the thought of parting with Pasquale.

I argued the unreasonableness of my attitude with myself, since there was no argument with Mary on this score. If she had had her way, we would have kept them all. Picayune, we had agreed, was the one to carry on the line, and she was satisfied with that. Then I came along, beating my breast not to let Pasquale go. The result was obvious. We kept them both.

After the seventh pup had found a happy home, our menagerie consisted of PJoe, Prudence, Picayune, Pasquale, six birds, and seven goldfish. Feeding time, while less like a zoo schedule, was still something to contend with. But things gradually calmed down and, except for a few moments of bedlam when the dogs were all let into the living room at once for the cocktail hour, it wasn't quite as much like a Roman coliseum as it had been before. Manners were slowly enforced, and we became almost a normal family . . . or as close to one, I felt, as we ever would be.

Joe was really a saint during the whole episode of the pups and became almost domesticated now that there were only two left, plus Prudence. He voluntarily discontinued his day-long haunt of the canyon to settle down at home, basking in endless bathings by Pasquale and Picayune, who, once they got him thoroughly clean and relaxed, proceeded to make themselves comfortable, setting their rear ends on his ample back.

The patience of Joe! I don't want to force the issue or labor the point, but Joe is really a biblical dog. His faith is as the faith of ten dogs; his patience is (with everyone except Mary, who is short on patience herself) eternal. He is a very democratic dog, single-purposed in his belief that all dogs are his brothers and stem from a common denominator. He is Hebraic in his lamentations in captivity, a psalmist to the full moon, a revelator of lost objects of his affections. He can beget and has begot with the best. His seed is dynastic.

Despite Joe's dynastic tendencies, Mary, for some reason obscure to me, has never taken an interest in the propagation of his breed. She has never shown the slightest interest in trying to better it or even change it. My feelings on the subject are that perhaps in his case well enough is best left alone. Why spoil perfection . . . or if I wanted to be cynical I could say why try to make a silk purse . . . and I won't belabor that point, either.

But Mary's pride as a dog breeder burst happily one day when a more successful if not more determined breeder told her that Picayune had real show possibilities and would indeed be a fine whatever the female equivalent of stud is in canine vernacular. Mary was persuaded to give up sole ownership of Picayune and to let her go live with this dog "pro" on the condition that the first white male puppy (in which fact she had never for a minute lost faith) would be ours.

Picayune bid us a tearful farewell and went into foreign parts to be trained and bred according to Hoyle rather than Mary. She made many visits to us over the years and where she had obviously gained in ring poise and points, as far as both of us were concerned, she had lost all personality. Perhaps the common quality Joe lends so generously to all he touches was missing.

Mary triumphed in the end, however, for Picayune did in truth have a pup, one pup, and a white one at that. This little hurricane of white fur came to visit us for a short while, for even Mary, who had counted her genes with genius had not counted on the perils of this pup to which the silent-movie Perils of Pauline were as a placid soap opera. Psean (pronounced "P Shawn") was let out for adoption and found a home with dear adoring friends who lavish on him all the loving attention he may not deserve but thinks he does—and so do they.

Things are still *status quo ante Psean* at our house, and fortunately a law is in effect that there can be only three dogs in one household, so for the moment we're safe. But I have never yet known a woman who could not circumnavigate a law, and I have my fingers crossed that the strong arm of that particular law will never get into an Indian-wrestling match with Mary—because I know who would win.

Chapter Six

I f for the moment I am persuaded to think that our lives are as full of animals as they can be or will be, perhaps I may be excused on the grounds that I am by choice a one-dog man, but in Prudence and Pasquale have reluctantly though happily become a three-dogger. Joe and I have made the adjustment to all newcomers and retained our mutual respect and, I think, dignity. The chains of love that bind us have grown stronger with the years, though I suspect that Charles A. Greene, Josephine, Prudence, her pups and grandpup are only the beginnings in this add-a-link chain; its strongest link is Mary—and weakest link is me. Joe remains untouched by her machinations and, while I grow more rubber-willed daily, he tempers his mettle with tenacity or, as Mary puts it, becomes more and more stubborn with each passing minute. Self-willfulness is a game that two can play, and Mary and Joe, to date, are undefeated champions, ready to take on all comers but brilliantly avoiding a play-off. Round after round I watch from the corner of my mind like a redundant referee, yesing and noing a contest I'm rarely called to judge.

When I'm forced to pull one or the other off the ropes or out of a clinch, the results are usually disastrous. Mary is determined to schedule Joe's freedom to her timetable, and Joe is equally convinced that the world is his freeway to be traveled as he sees fit. He is positively brilliant when it comes to breaking barriers imposed by her. While she is locking one door, he's out the other, and, though I will never again know an unsuspicious moment in her eyes, I have to confess that I often side with him, forgetting to close my doors behind me.

I love them both, and Mary has much right on her side. Joe is a bore about digging little lairs to lie in at the roots of some of our most prized plants. His bounding-outs quite often include escape for Prudence, who is a nose-to-the-ground explorer, never looking where she's going in a heavily trafficked neighborhood. Joe, while he's essentially clean, does shed enough hair annually to stuff a king-sized mattress. He does drink the water from newly watered flowerpot dishes, making it necessary to water house plants twice a week instead of once. And the one sure way he has of getting Mary's goat (the only animal she hasn't tried to domesticate) is to lift his leg in the kitchen, which of course causes her to lift her hand, reinforced with a newspaper, against him. The outcome teaches neither of them anything, and I have to clean up.

I can hardly say that Joe is defenseless against her. He's armed to the teeth with cunning little habits. At dinner he's inclined to get attention by putting a heavy, steel-clawed paw on Mary's bare leg, and the most severe reprimand, of giving a tidbit treat to Prudence instead of to him, only makes the demanding paw more ardent, and the reprimanding—this time, of me—louder: "Will you make that—dog of yours stop clawing me!"

He is always referred to as my dog, and he loves me, I think, but he's apt to take my reciprocated love for granted and go all out for Mary's, or, for that matter, that of anyone else who happens still to be eating. I'm a fast finisher of food, and Joe's immediate interest in me vanishes with the last forkful, to be directed on all, in turn, unto the last chance . . . and Mary is the slowest eater.

When love's magic smell is cast upon him, he fasts, and this aggravates Mary almost beyond endurance, for Prudence, whose appetite knows no bounds, absorbs both meals and loses her sprightly shape, so carefully guarded by Mary. To make up for her too short ears and too long nose, she does have the compensation of a slim waist. But this, too, goes when Joe's in love.

I know it would seem that Joe can't win, but don't you believe it. No war's lost until the enemy is completely demoralized, and, morally, Joe rearms himself daily with all the weapons at his disarming, delightful personality's disposal.

One of Mary's many complaints against Joe has to do with his odors. For the most part I find him sweet-smelling—like good old tweed. But he does take on odors. Just as he has a natural, protective coloring, being many-colored, he also picks up odors. For instance, if he gets to gobble up the leftovers of a lamb curry, he smells of curry for days.

Joe by any other name . . . would smell the same.

Sorry, I couldn't resist that. But my intention is not to enumerate the odors of Joe (which are many) but to put down some of the sweet talk and some of the invectives heaped upon the, to me, sterling character of this dog among dogs.

He has been most often referred to by Mary and by friends, who find him as charming as I do, as a Tijuana terrier. Now for those unfortunate readers who either are unaware of the charms of this particular border town, or are aware of them and don't find them charming, let me say that the breed of dog most populous in this thriving Baja California community can only be described as the terriers of Tijuana. Somewhere across some border they have a common ancestry in that multiple breed. They were Bedlington, Scottish, Airedale, fox, or some other kind to begin with—at least one feels so—but the result is a mix-master breed of all, and then some. A more bedraggled assortment would be hard to find, but, while they may not have much in common with any particular breed of terrier or other dog, they all have a distinctly Mexican charm. They have that wonderful South-of-the-Border ability to throw themselves down in any patch of sun or shade, according to their mood, and to remain there, despite world tensions, local rebellion, or momentous merriment. They are thin to the point of emaciation, but are much too mannerly to beg, preferring to fix you with wan eyes and let the chips fall where they may—if they do.

Most dogs thrive on petting almost as much as food, but in Mexico few people (including their owners) seem compelled to pet these. Perhaps the dust on their dingy coats does not call for this show of affection. Yet somehow one feels that they are greatly loved and as indispensable as dogs everywhere for the good of mankind . . . and for all the same reasons.

It is for these reasons that I have never taken umbrage at Joe's being called a Tijuana terrier. I have to admit that, except for the sometimes-silk sleekness of his coat and the obvious, well-fed rotundity of his stomach, he does have much in common with these, oh, so common, dogs. He can, and does, plop himself in the most precarious places, and if it were not for the almost psychic awareness he has for the presence of food within many yards of his hearing or smelling, he could indeed blend into the oblivion of dogdom, South of the Border, down Mexico way.

Then he has been likened unto a favorite character in my favorite comic strip, *Peanuts.* The strange little boy whose motto is: "Cleanliness is next to impossible," and who is called Pigpen. I take rather a dim view of this nomenclature, though Joe, like Pigpen, can indeed get dusty lying on a cement sidewalk. And his genius for finding a mud puddle in the midst of the worst drought in Southern California's history, while showing his undeniable inventiveness, does lead to some pretty severe disciplinary measures as far as coming into the house goes. But these, too, he accepts with mañana disconcern, knowing that if he hadn't done it today he would do it tomorrow.

"Stupid" is the one word most applied to Joe, but I will not allow it, and sympathetic fur bristles on my neck whenever I hear him called "stupid." Stupid he is not. Pigheaded, obstinate, slow . . . yes. But not stupid.

Joe makes me like him more just by being obstinate, pigheaded, slow. If he *is* stupid—that ugly word—then we would all be better off less bright. He gets what he wants, and do I . . . do you . . . ? When somebody calls, I run. He walks. When someone says: 'Do that,' I do it. He doesn't. Stupid?

Some time back, in his put-upon period of the acquisition of new dogs, a dog door had to be built—not so much for the dogs as for our help, who were rapidly revolting at opening another door to let the individual dog (or herds of dogs) out and in. Joe took one look at this swinging new contraption and refused to go out of it or come in by it. Stupid? I should say not. While the poodles rapidly learned that life was less inhibiting this way—and they could soon make up for the slight banging discomforture to their heads by the freedom given their overactive bodies—Joe balked at the whole ridiculous procedure. He had been used to being let out and let in as his due, at his command, and that's the way it was going to be. Four months of pushing, shoving, pulling, food tantalizingly left outside and in to coax . . . nothing worked. He still had to be let out personally and let in on demand. Then suddenly one day the silly game bored him and he used the dog door. Result? Four months of the most personal attention, his name on everybody's lips (and it doesn't make the slightest difference to Joe whether his name is preceded or followed by "dear" or "damn"). Haven't we all, in our maturity, wished that we were innocently, youthfully misunderstood to get attention? Of course.

I'll admit that this may sound like (or be construed as) stupidity. Well, just to prove my point, Joe learned to sit up like the poodles just a few weeks later than they did. After all, he was older, and, after all, there was something else involved. Food. Mind you, I shake my head a little when he is discovered sitting up for no reason whatsoever. But then, I suppose he reasons, Who can tell when some sweet tidbit will be forthcoming? Besides, he looks so cute sitting up all by himself. It's so complimentary to me, who taught him to do it in the first place.

I think that perhaps it would be best to get rid of the deprecations first. He went through a long period of being referred to as "that damned mutt" by a family whose reasons did have some justification.

They were close friends of mine, and Joe loved them with no more or less emotion than he shows for anyone who's good to him. Yet he must have thought more familiarly of them than of most people, because, suddenly one day, when two of them came to visit, he lifted his leg and let go identification on their shoes. He was, of course, properly reprimanded by them and told never to do it again. Since he'd never done it before, it seemed probable that he would never do it again. But he did. And that's when I first heard him called "that damned mutt."

Now these friends dearly loved Joe, so I had to come to the conclusion that his disconcerting lack of differentiation between their shoes and trees was annoying. Consequently I determined to follow Joe closely the next time they came to the house in the hopes of catching him in the act, since all he had to go on was their displeasure. I felt that, should he brook mine, he'd realize it wasn't the thing to do, would catch on, and cease. After all, he had never been known to identify on a human before. I don't know what strange notion made him think that these two could be signposts to or from anywhere. Anyway, I finally caught him at it and severely rubbed his nose on their shoes—which did seem a little extraordinary, but then, I really didn't know how else to go about curing him of what I didn't want to become a habit.

On their next few visits, not to put him to too great a test, I kept Joe in another part of the house. But when their parents and a group of people came to call one day without them, I forgot about Joe's predilection for their children's shoes and let him mingle with the company, as he loves to do.

There must have been ten people that day, but Joe deadlined for the parents of my friends and their shoes became part of the infinite complexity of his mysterious scent pattern. As far as they all were concerned, he became, permanently, that damned mutt!

If only Joe could be trained to do this to people I don't like. But no one has enough friends to let a damned mutt alienate them at his indiscretion! However, this was the only family he chose thus to baptize, and after he had further blessed the sister and one elderly aunt, he never did it again.

Joe is a creature of habit—who isn't?—and I'll admit that some of his habits are a touch annoying. Even I get annoyed when I find him cooling his belly in my fern-garden fish pond. There just isn't enough room in it for Joe and for the fish, whom I'm forever having to rescue from the drain basin below.

But the purpose of this chapter was to give the pros and cons of Joe, and so far it's been all cons. For every nasty thing someone else says about Joe I have antidotes of love words. Even if Joe pretends not to understand them, and they have been known to nauseate my family and friends, these words give me assurance that his feelings have not been hurt. If his feelings are as tough as his hide, they're not apt to be easily hurt, but I don't want to take any chances. So when he is called stupid or stubborn or dirty or messy, I run my hand over his silken brow and reassure myself that he is my Joselito, José, *mi hijo,* Jo. The effect of these Spanish terms of endearment on Joe is either a crocodile-like yawn or, if they end up with a kiss, a violent fit of sneezing.

Since he's matured he has grown progressively grayer at the temples, and recently I was embarrassed to hear myself call him Ronnie Joe when remarking on this distinctive coloring, which he shares with my favorite actor, the late great Ronald Colman. Whether that distinguished and delightful gentleman would have found this comparison flattering or not I'll never know. But believe me, it is a genuine expression of my admiration for both the man and the dog.

Anyone who won't admit that he speaks to his animal friend in special terms of endearment is a liar and a coward. This is the voice of love that needs and gets no answer, and therefore it needs no explanation. We make fools of ourselves over people and get caught at it, are rebuked or repulsed as often as we're accepted or as our protestations of love are returned. But to the silent world of animal adoration we can speak our piece and, even if we embarrass ourselves, we still can believe that they believe us or at least tolerate us—and they don't talk back.

Thus I feel that I have every right to use certain endearments with Joe. Perhaps no one has the right to make such a fool of himself—but don't we all?

Chapter Seven

I n the story of any one dog, the dogs of yesteryear must be remembered. Because of the time allotment, a man has many dogs in his life . . . a dog, only one man. My love for Joe represents a compilation of my love for others; each individual, each warmly remembered, and often more distinctly than any other fond event or particular period. Life could be the sum of the decades of our dogs.

Six to sixteen: Happy, a Boston bull terrier, in turn bouncy and sedate . . . my sister's dog and my inheritance when *the* man entered her life. Young marrieds are better off starting with *their* pet—not his or hers, as I have learned. I've seen many a hangover animal become a third, and unwanted, party (by one of them, at least) in a new marriage. My sister, realizing this, made her decision, and Happy stayed with me. She became my toy or, rather, replaced my toys.

Happy was a natural "ham," and in retrospect, I realize, so was I. Together we staged many a theatrical extravaganza . . . she patiently allowing me to dress her up in what was then my idea of history's characters, from Cleopatra to Mary, Queen of Scots. Authenticity was not part of my costume design as I improvised a bodice made of fur ear muffs and a beaded skirt fashioned from an undecorated lamp shade, topping it all off with dime-store earrings, weighing down her pointed ears. But she loved the attention and would play-act for hours, my silent partner in my first dramatic ventures.

When I was sixteen, this bug-eyed, pug-faced little ham of a co-star died of a punctured stomach after swallowing a chicken bone. She was missed and mourned by the entire household, but especially by me. Big as I was, I unashamedly shed many tears over her final exit.

I went to college the next year, and, since I was the last child of four, my parents decided not to have another dog. To my pleas they retaliated that I would be away and they just didn't feel like coping with a new pup. So for three years our house was dogless, and on my vacation visits I was too busy to wish it otherwise. Mother and Dad had had their generations of pets throughout their own lives and their children's, so I'm sure that the quiet of a home without either was welcome, if startlingly lonely at first.

Their time of peace was to be short-lived. Senior year in college, my roommate and I, settling down from three hectic years of calling Prohibition's bluff, spent many quiet weekends with his parents who lived nearby. In their lovely New England home I fell in love with my first dachshund, a shiny stovepipe of a dog with saddle-colored spots. She squirmed her way into my heart, reviving bitter remembrances I had of the mistreatment accorded the breed during World War I. My home town was half German and half French, and feeling ran so high between these good Americans that spite killings of these adorable dogs were continually reported and deplored in the papers. My family was shocked at such adolescent retaliations of nationalistic feelings and transmitted their sympathy to me. I had never really allowed myself to think of dachshunds in terms of affection, lest these brutalities should ever happen again.

But all that was long past when I met Lisa. Our rapport was instant and grew, over weekends, into one of those flattering relationships wherein absence obviously made her heart grow fonder. Assurances by her owners that Lisa didn't accord such an elaborate welcome to everyone only made her flattery get her anywhere she wanted to go with me.

Lisa was mated with an excellent dachshund gent, sporting lineage as distinguished as hers, and in time I was given one of their daughters who became Lisa the Second. For the last three months of my senior year she lived a cloistered existence in Harkness Quadrangle at Yale University, then traveled with me to St. Louis, Missouri, to live with my parents.

Since the sweet gray gull of youth had at long last feathered out to white and now must fly the stormy oceans of maturity in search of support, I necessarily deposited Lisa at home, where she was lovingly received, and left for a job as an apprentice teacher in a summer camp school back East—a job that required my wet-nursing some of the richest delinquents on the Eastern seaboard.

My parents kept me duly posted on Lisa's escapades, and between the lines of their letters I could read that, past resolutions to the contrary, they were once again happily dogbound.

In time, Lisa produced six puppies, and Mother and Father were so enchanted they kept three. On a visit home I saw why. This comedic quartette, starring Lisa and her three little stumpy-legged stovepipes, could have given the brethren Marx a run for their performing money. Family and friends scrambled in to share the cocktail hour every evening. It became an elaborate ritual, executed with elegance by the hosts and partakers of the hosts, alike. Lisa came first, then Schnick, then Hansie, and, lastly, grunting like an overstuffed sausage, Vicky. This last little pig was the favorite of Ida, our cook. She overfed Vicky's disposition, which was dispeptic to begin with, and ruined her figure forever.

Each of the dogs had to sit up for his treat, and all of them made it with different success. Lisa, who had spawned the group, could hold the pose only a few seconds, melting into a shapeless heap the minute she got hers. Schnick had marvelous manners and would eat his sitting up. Perhaps he learned that by staying up he got an extra one from Dad. Hansie snapped his, went down on all fours to look for invisible crumbs, and then sprang back into position for more.

But it was Vicky who delighted all with her labors, trying

to get into a sitting position. She was so fat her front legs had little leverage to push her bulk up in the air, and, once up, her hind legs completely disappeared under her round, pink, pear-shaped belly. Only her long tail, sticking straight out behind, held her up—and not for long. If she wasn't fed at once, it was too late, and the whole arduous exercise began again.

This comedy team cheered my parents' declining years. They performed the miracle all loved and loving pets perform of keeping age alive to life. Let no man turn his thoughts from other living things, if he would watch the years go by with joy in the experience of growing old.

During these years my pursuits had taken me far from home, and in London, England, I embarked on a theatrical career. A year in a London flat, shared with two young English gentlemen, brooked no levity, such as owning a dog, on the part of an American. The flat was on Baker Street, where Sherlock Holmes resided, but dogs were definitely not the order of the day in my time there, even if *he* maintained a kennel of bloodhounds. Baker Street is a busy thoroughfare between two great commercial centers, and the little parks that dot the surrounding neighborhood hardly support a man in search of exercise, let alone a dog. In England people keep dogs in the country and, except for two French street-walkers who sported silver foxes on their necks and police dogs on leash, I don't remember many dogs in London.

But someone made the mistake of telling me that Selfridge's Department Store, at one end of Baker Street, had a great pet shop. As a matter of fact, it was boasted that Selfridge's could supply you with anything from an elephant to American coffee . . . two equally rare commodities in London, 1935.

Perhaps because my English friends had been so kind to me, I really didn't realize that I was lonely without a pet of some kind. I had not only forgotten that I had almost never been without an animal friend . . . I'd almost forgotten that I was an American. When these two realizations dawned on me, I thought that I'd better do something about them both, and quickly. Well, what more logical way than to accept the challenge of Selfridge's and have a look around the pet shop, and, while I was about it, have a cup of coffee, too. Selfridge himself was another transplanted American, but permanently, which I had no intention of becoming, love London and the British as I did.

My flat-sharers were reservedly terrified at the thought of what I might bring back to live with us all. I had already flooded their lives with stray actors and actresses from the famous little Gate Theatre, where I made my debut on the stage. While the prospect of more actresses was delightful to them both, the idea of our little flat housing a Selfridge-purchased elephant (and I'm sure they thought that their crazy American boarder was just crazy enough to make a down payment on one) was really too much.

They allowed as how they would not mind a cat, because

it could roam the large block of connected roof tops the flat let out on. However, they looked apprehensive as I went out the door.

Luckily, for my roommates, Selfridge's happened to be fresh out of elephants, so I perused the various cages, and in one I met my future pet. He was *semi*-exotic, and that's what made him so desirable. Siamese cats were fairly new on the world pet stage at that time, so the sight of a blue-eyed cat was somewhat startling to a Missouri boy, coming across one for the first time in London. Perhaps I just never had moved in the upper echelon of pet owners, or St. Louis was slow to get around to accepting this foreign breed. Anyway, I couldn't remember ever having seen a pair of blue eyes (and slightly crossed blue eyes, at that) stare out of any of the thousands of cats I had come face to face with so far in my life.

He wasn't a kitten, this new-found friend. He was already well on his way to being a cat. But there was still an awkward-ness about him that was irresistible, and something else—his rear end was a great deal higher than his front end, and the fur covering one part had nothing to do with that covering the rest. His face was typically Siamese—tawny fox, shading to black at his ear tips; black whiskers and a shiny black nose. But from about an inch below his neck to the base of his tail the fur became gradually more and more striped until his rump was pure tabby. Then the stripes narrowed again, go-ing up his tail till at the tip he was once more a black-tipped Siamese.

He was christened Albert the Good, not only because I had just made a success, playing the part of the prince consort in the Gate Theatre production of *Victoria Regina*, but also because Albert was really a good cat. He had all the best cat qualities. The rear half-tabby balanced the front half-Siamese, toning down the latter's impetuous and often tempestuous whimsey and brightening up the former's sometimes too phlegmatic attitude of: "I'm a cat. See that I get all the attention due me."

When the time came for me to leave England and go back to my native land, there was much discussion about Albert. I knew that he would have a good home in Baker Street (he was definitely invited to stay), but I had become deeply attached to him and decided to take him back to New York with me. It was a sad moment for all of us, but, after all, he was my cat and part of a wonderful period of my life that he alone could keep alive and out of memory's inevitable grave.

As a going-away gift my flat-mates presented Albert with a beautiful wicker basket, decorated with his initial in royal-purple velvet glued on a wooden "A" by the loving hands of one of their girl friends.

Albert took to the basket not at all, and carrying him in it almost made me seasick. He circled and paced and wiggled and scratched. He had never been confined since I took him from the cage in Selfridge's. I felt like a murderer or a kidnapper as I carried the rocking, rolling, swinging basket down the street to the car in which a friend was driving me to Southampton to catch the boat. And the deep, agonizing yowls coming from the very soul of that semi-Siamese (whose voice was *all* Siamese) assured onlookers that I was, indeed, a deep-dyed villain and should immediately be reported to the Royal Society for the Prevention of Cruelty to Animals.

Once at sea, Albert turned out to be a sailor—a show-off sailor—and an old salt, for sure. It was his daily pleasure during the trip to New York, even in the most horrid weather and roughest seas of November, to race assorted human diehards as they took *their* daily exercise around the deck, while I sat by, sickly resigned to the certain knowledge that of his nine lives none of them would be lost at sea!

He was part and parcel of one of my young life's interesting episodes. As a result of my appearance in the London company, the great impresario Gilbert Miller had hired me to play Prince Albert opposite Helen Hayes's Victoria in the New York production of *Victoria Regina*. Mr. Miller justifiably refused to pay my passage back to the States, since I was an American. But what he hadn't realized was that I was broke and was hardly able to scrape passage money together to get back in time for rehearsals. I went to England third class but had to return steerage. It didn't bother me, and one advantage it gave me was proximity to Albert, my cat. His quarters were practically next to mine, and since the ship was half empty and the stewards very lenient, he was allowed extra visiting hours with me in my cabin and more time on deck—and on a higher-class deck than he ever could have aspired to in the season.

The weather was so bad we were delayed eight hours and docked about 8:00 P.M. instead of midmorning. My paraphernalia consisted of a minimum amount of clothes, two heavy packages of precious art books, a long string of shoes—and Albert. All of this was duly inspected by Customs, including Albert, who passed the quarantine, and I checked into a low-priced hotel.

The next morning, when I reported to Mr. Miller, all hell broke loose. He angrily blasted me for not meeting the press who had come to interview me when the *Aquatania* docked. Who the hell did I think I was—*Garbo*?

Of course, the press had gone into first class to meet Helen Hayes's new leading man, and, of course, I'd been in steerage and never the twain did meet. It took some placating of Mr. Miller's volatile temper, but all ended well and Albert and I set up modest housekeeping and went on with the show.

After the play was established as a hit, we moved into a fairly snappy, one-room apartment on lower Park Avenue, where Albert proceeded to crochet the furniture into an interesting, over-all terry-cloth texture. I lived with Albert's shredded furnishings until *Victoria* finally closed and I decided to move into another place. The crochet job set me back three hundred dollars.

My new apartment was on West Fifty-third Street, between Fifth Avenue and what is now (but never referred to as) the Avenue of the Americas—Sixth Avenue. The old "el" turned the corner there, and under it huddled a dozen cozy dark bars, restaurants, and shops, the owners of which were good neighbors and friends. You really didn't have to walk more than four blocks to sustain life in the most charming way. Everybody was everybody's friend. We all knew all about each other, and Albert and I settled into this new life, happily comparing it to our ancient life in London on Baker Street.

The apartment was one good-sized room in the rear of a brownstone on the street level. It had a garden, an ideal spot for Albert's toilette and for my horticultural prowess. With the aid of an old bathtub, sunk in the ground, and some flagstones, I made a pool, the goldfish inhabitants of which made wonderful watching for the cat. Discarded pine trees and ornamental shrubs, picked out of rubbish cans in the dead of night from wealthier sections of town, thrived under our loving care, and the garden became quite famous to all the neighbors higher up in the surrounding buildings. Kirsten Flagstad lived in an apartment hotel on the next street, and often glorious music trickled down into our garden from her open window, twelve stories up.

Albert took to the roof tops once again, and once again developed a devoted coterie of admirers. Our new neighborhood also included a pet shop. Nothing attracts more attention in New York than a pet-shop window, and my nose mark was not missing among the dozens regularly established thereon. Sooner or later I knew that a wistful pair of dog eyes would stare up at me out of the straw and Albert and I would have a new roommate.

Two days after I had opened in a terrible flop called *The Lady Has a Heart* (the critics didn't), I wandered down Sixth Avenue in that critically induced state of amnesia in which all actors forget themselves when connected with a failure. In my lostness I was drawn to the pet-shop window, and there, of course, was something more lost than I was. A brown-patched, white English bulldog puppy reeled around the cage on his gnarled legs. His jaw was as far out as mine in a determination not to let life get him down. His price was twenty-five dollars. I had twenty-five dollars, but I had no right to spend it with the imminent closing of the play staring me in the face. But everyone has a way (or many ways) of counteracting the blues. In order to get out of the dumps, there are many steps to walk up, and most of the ones I know of, not only for myself but others, are made of money.

Women buy new hats or perfume. Men get a haircut and blow themselves to a shampoo, face and scalp massage, and manicure. Some people get drunk. Others go off on a trip. I have two steps: art and animals. Art always cheers me up, even if I can't or don't buy it. It gives me courage to see the creative products of others.

Animals cheer me because they are so dependent on man, and most men are completely willing to take them on as dependents. Animals are a reminder that something needs us and that we are capable of fulfilling that need. It's often damned difficult to return affection to another human being, but one does it without thinking to an animal.

Enter Johnny Bulldog!

When Johnny first became a member of the "family," Albert-the-Good lived up to his name. He decided right off that Johnny was the one animal in the world for him. The patience of Albert toward that pup I have never seen equaled (save for the already-described patience of this book's hero, Joe). But, alas, it was not a permanent attitude. Patience and pup were synonymous with Albert, but when pup became dog, Albert became all cat, and the proverbial "fight like cats and dogs" went out of the realm of proverb into fact. One memorable bout finally resulted in Albert's packing up his loyalty to me and leaving home. I'd hoped, in the long days of searching and inquiring around the neighborhood, that it really was only a temporary flare-up of ancient enmity, but my hopes were dashed by a sweet (though anonymous) note left in my mailbox. The contents assured me that Albert had a new and happy home, and the writer generously offered to return Albert to me if I got rid of my dog. This was downright spooky—no address, no name—with the additional weird statement that the writer "would know" when and if Johnny was ousted. For a time, after receiving the note, every patron of the neighborhood market, the local pub, and the Chinese laundry became a focal point for my impolite stares. I had to make a decision before I became the counterpart of a village idiot.

Unquestionably a dog is truly dependent. Unlike a cat, he can't roam the roof tops for ablutions. For various reasons he can't come and go as he pleases in a city. There was only one decision I could make: resign myself to life without Albert and *with* Johnny. And this I did.

That fall Johnny and I drove to St. Louis for a visit. The family dachshunds hated him and he hated them. Johnny was becoming a problem. He needed space for his bull-doggedness and a friend of my sister offered him a home on a big farm. Another tough decision because, though fundamentally, I believe that dogs don't belong in cities, sentimentally, I guess I just hate to be without one. Now here was a case where a big brute of a dog had to be led around a concrete jungle to scratch in tiny plots of earth for any comfort whatsoever. Why shouldn't he have a chance to roll in the grass, scratch his backside against a tree, chase birds, sit in a creek, let his nostrils fill with all the sweet odors of real life? Why should he have to pay the penalty of my whim to have a dog in New York? Why should he suffer the restrictions of that kind of life or the unavoidable loneliness I had to put him through because of the nature of my work?

So Johnny became a farm dog, and I kept up with his happiness in his new life through many postcards. He made a new friend in the person of a Shetland pony and was having the time of his life chasing chickens and rabbits, none of which he could ever catch on those stumpy, bowed legs of his.

I made a vow, then and there, never to put myself or an animal through all this again until I had a home, a yard, and the kind of life not only a dog, but a man, should have.

And I kept it. Actually, the vow was easily kept, since pursuing a living in the theater found me hitting the road, living in hotels, then returning to New York to more hotels or small apartments, designed to cramp my own six-foot-four. Consequently a four-legged *anything,* save a nomadic field mouse, would have been out of the question.

It wasn't until I was forced to make up my mind that my profession could possibly afford me a permanent home and that it would have to be in California, and Hollywood, that I felt I could resume a life with animals. The minute I felt that I had that home I knew it wouldn't be a real one without a dog. Home life depends on how much life is in the home. Dogs make a home alive, and at this moment in my life my home's alive with dogs, all of whom I love, but one special one is as dear to me as life itself . . . my boy Joe.

Chapter Eight

Although Joe, snoring away at my feet at the moment, has always commanded the at-home center stage, I have taken my share of on-stage professional bumps from those inevitable scene stealers, the "trained" performing animals.

I don't know whether oysters can be considered in the legitimate cast of such animals as I've played with, but my first experience with other than people on a stage was with them. It was in Schnitzler's great comedy *Anatole* at the little Gate Theatre in London. One scene was a wild dinner party, and since the stage was right in the audience's lap, it was difficult to fake the food. Oysters were part of the dialogue and the menu, so real oysters they had to be—not halves of grapes or any other substitute.

It seems that oysters are terribly expensive in England (at least the good ones are), and since all Gate Theatre productions were done on a shoestring, we were not given those delicious Ostend or Whitstable varieties, but the kind that are sold "incognito" by street vendors.

Opening night, in the gusto of the first performance, the three of us involved in the scene ate two dozen between us, and if the notices the next day were bad (which, indeed, they were), they had nothing on the oysters. We were all violently ill.

In my theatrical experience nothing has ever topped the dejection of the three of us the second night of that play. Bad notices and bad oysters are guaranteed to build any actor up to a big letdown, and you don't have to add the bad notices.

My first lesson in how to handle animal charms on stage came from Miss Helen Hayes in the New York production of *Victoria Regina.* A scene took place, after my demise in the play, that involved Queen Victoria's historic Pomeranian, Mop. He arrived on the scene, led on by her beloved friend, John Brown. The oh's and ah's from the audience were to be expected, and were expected by the very wise Miss Hayes, who let it all happen, and then, before resuming the scene, saw to it that Mop was carefully shielded from the audience's doting view by her voluminous widow's weeds. Mop had his second moment of triumph as he was led off at the end, and he took full advantage of it by fluffing himself out to his full, minute majesty and snortling off. Whereupon Miss Hayes, using a great actress's know-how, envisioned in that dog the happy memories of her marriage and completely recaptured the audience by a flood of tears and the tender words: "Oh, Albert, Albert."

In my first motion picture, *Service De Luxe,* I didn't have to contend with animals to achieve oblivion, but with the next greatest threat a straight leading man can have—the comedian. In that one I had three of them to contend with: Helen Broderick, Charlie Ruggles, and Mischa Auer—any one of whom could have made me disappear, and though they were all souls of kindness to me, I disappeared.

Early in a desperate climb to some sort of movie prominence I came up against my first animals, a whole litter of King Charles spaniels, and I was playing King Charles. But my competition was not the spaniels, who were indeed adorable, but the enormous bosoms of the young lady who played Nell Gwyn. They were of such robust and luscious proportions and her dress cut so low that in our big scene, in which we fondled the puppies on a great bed, she leaned over them so far the censors cut the scene out of the picture. Never underestimate the power of a woman.

During the long run of *Angel Street* on Broadway I lived in a midtown Manhattan hotel that forbade animals on the premises, so I cast around for some object for my affections and found it in the charming goat so prominently cast in the next-door revival of *Porgy and Bess*.

I doubt if the public ever realizes how much of an actor's life takes place in those dingy, dirty alleys leading from the street to the stage entrance of most theaters. To backstage visitors they are the last part of the last mile in which you screw up your courage to go behind the scenes. They are guaranteed to dispel any illusion the play may have created.

But it is down those damp corridors that the actor has to exit from the world of reality and enter the one of make-believe. It is also in these dust-deep and often highly scented canyons that the actors must retire for a breath of fresh air between acts and between scenes, since most dressing-room windows are hermetically sealed.

Angel Street played on Forty-fifth Street between Broadway and Eighth Avenue, and the alley that led back to the stage entrance of the Golden Theatre also let in on another theater, the Majestic, which housed *Porgy and Bess,* its audience entrance on Forty-fourth Street. It was therefore a more commodious alley than most, serving as it did two theaters. The life in it also had a little more liveliness as our small cast became friendly with the much larger population of Catfish Row. We fraternized between acts, and I was fortunate enough to catch hundreds of renditions of "Summertime" and "Bess, You Is My Woman Now." During the hot summer months it was very jolly in the alley, and an ice-cream vendor, with an eye for business, even found his way back there.

New York theaters were not air-conditioned at that time, at least ours weren't, and backstage was terribly stuffy. *Porgy and Bess* had at least fifty people in the cast and one goat, and since even one goat has a way with it in a close interior, Porgy's goat was kept out in the alley between scenes. He didn't help the atmosphere of that alley much either, but he was a pretty goat and very friendly and was a natural receptacle for all leftover tidbits all of the actors and stagehands in both companies saved from their coffee breaks and sandwich snacks. We even brought him special treats of celery, radishes, and fruits from Sardi's and other nearby eating establishments.

It was in an off-stage moment of feeding the goat that one of my most embarrassing stage experiences happened. The Eskimo Pie man set up shop near the goat in the alley. One hot summer evening, visiting them both and having found that I just had time for half an Eskimo Pie, with the goat enjoying the other half, I had gone out to indulge us in this customary treat. The pies were particularly well frozen that night, and, biting into it, I dislodged the cap on a front tooth.

That night the goat got the whole pie, as I fled into the theater to see what I could do to replace the tooth for the next scene, and until I could have it replaced at the dentist's the next day.

The cap itself was of no use, so I plugged up the hole with a wad of adhesive tape. It seemed fairly permanent and wouldn't look too bad from the front.

The scene still to be played required a subtle pursuit of my unhappy stage wife, accusing her of having been searching my desk while I was away. It also called for me to sip a glass of milk at one point and then bellow another accusation at her in a sharp staccato shout like that of a gun.

The milk dissolved what little hold the adhesive had on my other teeth, and, instead of the vocal report designed to make her confess her guilt, a wad of tape shot from my mouth and across the stage, hitting her square on the cheek.

The rest of the scene was helplessly lisped and limped to an undramatic conclusion. There's nothing more innocuous than trying to be menacing with a drooping lip and a missing tooth.

While I could hardly blame Porgy's goat for this minor disaster, our friendship did fall off since I'd learned to be wary of between-scene visits in the alley, and to this day I carefully test an Eskimo Pie before I bite into it.

There is one kind of animal that doesn't like me, and I must admit I don't much like it. It's a question of mutual distrust. The horse and I just don't see eye to eye.

In the first place the top of a horse and my bottom don't fit. My legs are too long and my torso too short—in short I look ridiculous on top of a horse and I suspect that it feels ridiculous under me. Maybe the situations should be reversed.

I think that if I were ever put on the couch to find out why I don't like horses, much resentment would bubble up against my family, friends, and especially against men who run boys' summer camps. My family made me learn to ride simply because it was done by young men in our set, and that to me is the lowest reason I can think of for doing anything or making someone else do something. My friends have always kidded me about how I look on a horse. Much of my extreme youth was spent in misery because of impolite references to myself and a sack of potatoes. I think I've lived it down, but I still find it hard to be polite to the boys, now men, who made those references.

I'll admit that riding can be fun. At the age of ten, in a Western summer camp, in spite of the discrepancies between the horse's shape and mine, I learned to enjoy the brisk canter, but the slow, long, walk or trot or whatever they do that jars your coccyx into your cranium—that is for cowboys and jockeys, not for me.

John Stahl, one of the great, old-time movie directors, with whom I did four pictures, almost succeeded in kidding me out of my horse-versus-Price aversion. In the first version of *Forever Amber* I was cast as the friend of the hero and had to ride a great deal. Mr. Stahl used to shout over the P.A. system: "For God's sake, don't look so stupid on that horse, Vincent, look as though you liked it."

My feeble "But I don't like it, Mr. Stahl" was lost in the clatter of hoofs as we charged down the hills, but I was so determined to make it at least look good I usually ended up the only one whose hat, wig, or cape hadn't blown off or whose horse hadn't been brought to its knees by a swinging sword.

I've learned to ride and I've learned not to look like a sack of potatoes in front of the camera. Trainers tell me that I ride well, but I still feel that the horse is the master and I'm on his back only by his leave.

I do, however, get along fine with apes and have worked sack of potatoes in front of the camera. Trainers tell me that they like my voice and that because I treat them as people they like me. Well, it's easy to do, since some of them are people and easier to work with than some—people, I mean actors.

On an Art Linkletter show I worked with the famous chimp whose painting won a prize in a people's art show. I guess they thought that my love of art—painting, that is— would make us a funny pair, but I really felt that the chimp had great talent, and if he could only have been persuaded from eating more paint than he put on the canvas, he might have turned out something accidentally interesting. After all, they have the intelligence of children and children are great artists, but children can use real paints, and ape paint has to be edible.

The most talented chimp I knew was on another Linkletter show. He was an adorable youngster and very well trained. He loved to smoke cigarettes, and the last gag of the plot, wherein I bragged that I could teach a monkey to do anything Mickey Rooney's son Teddy could do, involved a cigarette.

The chimp was supposed to mix me a martini and then reach for a cigarette and light it while I answered the question: "What brand does he smoke?" with "He thinks for himself." He had done every trick with remarkable alacrity, but here he balked. The martini was mixed, the olive put in the glass, but nothing would induce him to take the cigarette.

In filmed television this is pretty expensive temperament, and while his trainer was having a nervous breakdown, the chimp was happily drinking the fake martini. Then suddenly the trainer leaped to the rescue. In angry tones he asked what kind of cigarettes were in the prop box . . . some ordinary brand.

They were immediately exchanged for a mentholated pack, and this time the chimp mixed the martini, handed it to me, took the cigarette, lit it, and had a happy smoke.

The chimps were charming but impersonal. Whatever affection they gave me quickly dissolved when their trainer appeared, but I did once develop a one-sided romance with another animal—a camel. It seems that camels become enormously attached to certain individuals and not necessarily their owners or caretakers, and this happened to me on a desert location for a film called *Baghdad*.

All through one week's filming in the blistering sun, take after take was being ruined by the inhuman howls of a lady camel. No one could make her stop, and the furious reprimand by the sound man to the animal owner brought out the news that the camel must have fallen in love with one of the cast. It couldn't be anyone she was used to, because it had never happened before and the crew had been around the animals for a week before we arrived. Since there were only three men, including myself, in the company and lady camels fall only for human men, it must be one of us.

Unbeknownst to me, the undignified suggestion was made that the three of us be presented to the camel in question. I was elsewhere when my two co-workers were paraded before her. I walked onto the set at the end of this unlikely spectacle. They apparently had caused her no emotional upset whatsoever, but the moment I appeared the great lumpy beast gave forth with the most disturbing screams of passionate anguish. I was the object of her affection and also the friendly derision of the entire company, but the film was able to continue by eliminating this camel from any scene I was in.

One evening after work I thought I'd just see if my camel appeal was for real, so I casually sauntered by their corral. Sure enough the lusty love call rang through the evening calm and I strode away, smug in the knowledge that it's not every man who could find a camel willing to walk a mile for him.

Once I was offered a TV show that intrigued me, for the *deus ex machina* of the story was an extraordinary cat called Sheila. I accepted the script because I couldn't stand not to see how a cat could do so many remarkable tricks. Sheila had to be fierce, loving, at once utterly feline and almost human. Cats, as I knew them anyway, are long on independence and short on patience. They just don't have many tricks up wherever cats have tricks.

As Sheila was cast, she was a lovely, tawny-yellow, tiger-striped cat and scene after scene she went through her remarkable repertoire. She kissed me, bit me, frightened me, purred or yowled on command. I was amazed. But soon the cat had to be let out of the bag, and much to my amazement Sheila turned out to be eight identical cats. Each one had her specialty and, as a matter of fact, three of her were hes.

In another picture, called *The Long Night*, I played the part of a down-beat magician night-club entertainer. My prize exhibit was a sextet of the cutest dogs ever to be so beautifully choreographed into an act. To get them to work with me as well as they did with their trainer, I had to rehearse with them for two weeks prior to the beginning of the picture. The dogs, two tiny toy poodles, one black, one white, two miniature poodles, one brown, one black and white, and two fox terriers, brown and white, and terribly talented all of them, were tolerant of me from the beginning. With their trainer by my side they would go through their paces and after two days it seemed to me that if he were to step out of the way I could carry on alone. But that's not the way it works. I asked him to try it and found that I could get them through two of their paces alone, but their attention wandered after that and so did they—all over the stage looking for him.

At the end of the two weeks I could get them all the way through the act alone, but only after I'd learned thoroughly what he told me—that you have to talk tough to them and be disciplinarily tough with them, too. The minute I let my heart melt at their winsomeness, they were out of the schoolroom and into a prolonged play period with all the crew and the dozens of visitors who continually crowded the set to watch this stupid actor try and train six brilliant pups.

About the middle of the rehearsal period my chances of ever getting them to work with me looked so slim that I rubbed some hamburger on my shoelaces. But they were way ahead of me. They sniffed the lovely odor haughtily and ran off to look for the real stuff, which was always forthcoming from their beloved trainer.

However, it did work out wonderfully well and, though my respect for the talent of those animals reached fever pitch, my admiration for their trainer's patience hit heavenly altitudes.

Probably the most heart-warming thing about the whole episode was those few minutes when I'd first get back home and be met by an anxious Joe, who went over my trouser legs like a vacuum cleaner, to make sure (I like to think) that none of my love for him had been purloined.

If my life with other animals reads, chronologically, somewhat *non sequitur*, I can only say that prodding one's memory creates this. Dig deeply in one place, unearth one of memory's treasures, and an immediate cave-in may result. Dig out, and you discover that you're on a path different from the one you'd planned. Or, in the Freudian sense, call it free association. And it's Joe's fault that I am suddenly stricken philosophic. I have just read a few paragraphs aloud, actor-style, so that I might hear what I've thought. At one point Joe looked at me long and hard, from his curled position on my sleeping foot, and emitted the most elaborate of yawns. I refuse to accept this gesture as a critique. Perhaps he's urging me to get on with *his* story, the egomaniac, but since he's flopped back to sleep, I'll digress from the lovable lump long enough to unearth another memory, particularly vivid because it began at Easter time—and Easter has always been a favorite time of mine. I love the story of the Resurrection; I love lilies and I love spring. However, this particular Easter, 1948, found me without my full zest for its beauty of color and connotation. There were still hung-over vestiges of hurt from the preceding Christmas, when my son and I ceased living under the same roof. He now lived with his mother in a little house about ten blocks from where Joe and I shared temporary bachelor-apartment quarters. Well, "bachelor-apartment" is a bit too chic. It was actually a garage and another garage that had been made into a room with a shower, toilet, and tiny cooking closet. It was at the end of a dead-end street, and the tiny, semi-enclosed garden looked out on fields—the last fields to exist in that part of fast-growing Los Angeles.

The hardest times were the holidays. *Everyone* really tried to make them festive and gay for the boy and probably went overboard, bringing too much and too forced a holiday spirit into his life those few hectic days. We went berserk, buying toys and candy; decorating his mother's house with flowers; and friends, sensing the difficulty, added more of everything. Their house looked like an Easter-parade float. One rich friend ordered a four-foot bunny that frightened even her when she met it face to face, and she finally had to give her consent to storing it in the garage because it terrified every child who saw it.

I had sent flowers and prepared a couple of dozen very fancy eggs in my little apartment, and was especially proud of a very large sugar egg I'd found that, when you looked in one end of it, contained a glorious scene in the life of Hansel and Gretel. I was doing some last-minute rummaging around town for added trinkets when I passed a ten-cent-store window full of baby chicks. I passed it, but the temptation was too great, so I doubled back and in, and came away with two chirping little peepers and full instructions as to their care. A warning had been given by the shopkeeper that their chances for survival were very thin, but that I had selected carefully and the ones I had picked were certainly two of the healthiest of the lot.

I'm always intrigued by my nonsensical concern with picking out of a bunch of things that look exactly alike the ones that somehow I feel are the best and belong to me. It's that same crazy urge or superstition, or whatever it is, that makes me open a Bible in a hotel room, hoping for some great happenstance spiritual word of advice. More often than not, I hit a long passage of begats and begots, which contain little inspiration other than the fact that procreation is the highest aim of life.

Of course my chicks were the hit of the day. Who could resist them? I gave my boy the complete list of instructions and promised that I'd come every day and help him see to it that they reached maturity.

I kept my promise, and they did. In miraculously short time the fluff disappeared and feathers sprouted out of the quill cases. From yellow peepers they grew into little yellow-and-white chickens, and then they stopped growing. There was an endless period when they didn't change at all. Then, all of a sudden, their shapes began to change. They began to fill out and new feathers appeared, this time multicolored, and it dawned on me that they were not ordinary chickens but bantams. Another metamorphic period elapsed, and it dawned on me that they were bantam *roosters*! Wonderful, wobbly combs appeared on their heads, and great plumes of iridescent feathers sprang from their tails. Miraculously, they had reached their full size and their determination to rule the household—all at once. No longer did they *have* to

2

be fed. They *demanded* to be fed! At every opportunity they marched into the house, let forth a blasting crow, perched themselves on a chair back or on top of a cupboard, and announced that they were hungry.

They were the most imperious birds I'd ever seen and extremely beautiful. Each week or so some new color appeared and the feathers grew more luxurious and longer. One of them developed a three-foot tail by the time the miracle was complete.

My boy, who had adored the whole cycle of their development, began to be a little intimidated by their haughtiness, for, instead of their being his pet chickens, he soon became their pet boy. They took him over completely. They would roost in the trees, and when he went out to play they'd pounce down on him with shrieks of delight and ride around the yard on his shoulders. The more he put up with it, the more they took advantage of him, until he became a boy with two permanent rooster-epaulets on his shoulders and with no freedom whatsoever. The only other person they liked was me, and we must have made a pretty peculiar father-and-son team, decorated as we were, at every visit, by two fancy, full-plumed bantam roosters.

The more we tolerated their advances, the more demanding they got and the rougher their play became. They would pick at our ears, and one day they drew blood by an overeager peck at one of the boy's more tender ones.

That was the end for his mother. They had to go. But the

question was—where? What do you do with two feisty bantam cocks in Beverly Hills?

I had known that the moment was coming when they would have to find another home, because (from various reports to me) dawn kept getting earlier and earlier—for them, at least—and their voices kept getting louder and louder. They could be heard a block away, and were. The neighbors let it be known in a formal petition signed by ten of them. It was a politely phrased petition, but it allowed as how they were all hard-working people who needed their sleep and didn't need this extra reminder to be up and about their business. The old alarm clock, they rationalized, could be gagged, pushed aside, or turned off. But not the roosters.

So it was decided that they should move in with me. My son was in tears, lest they should be lost to him forever, so I had to promise to take good care of them and report daily on their welfare in their new surroundings. I took Joe off to stay with friends until the roosters' housing could be permanently arranged.

It was one devil of a job catching them, for they must have sensed that something was up. The day decided upon for their removal they decided to break their habit of descending on us from their tree, and no amount of coaxing could get them down. I finally climbed into the branches and, after a noisy and feather-flying fight, got them down and stuffed into the cage I had bought, which, while it accommodated their bodies, left no room for the pride of tail feathers that spurted out of the wire in all directions.

I had a tiny English Austin at the time, as a wartime gas saver, so they were crammed into the single seat next to the driver's, and we started off while the petitioning neighbors looked on with delight. Such a carful of feathers and noise had never been heard or seen in Beverly Hills. While I could see the humor of it, I took a dim view of my role.

My little garden had a tree in the center of it. I had built a four-foot fence around it in anticipation of one day beautifying it a bit. Now I knew that those dreams would never be realized. The bleak view out my window would be bleaker as a chicken yard, and indeed it became so. In a mere day's time, the roosters took over completely. The grass became their picking garden; the few new shrubs I'd put out were in-between-meal snacks; the earth was pocked with dozens of little ditches for them to nestle in, and the tree was their private domicile. From it they could spy me coming and lie in wait to pounce on me, no matter what time of day or night I was foolish enough to come home.

Dawn came up like thunder for everyone in my neighborhood now, and I came up for some fancy dressing-downs by baggy-eyed inhabitants, whose morning sleep had been rendered nonexistent.

One rooster's tail was so long he had to move to a higher branch to keep it from dragging on the ground, where cats could catch at it—for no cat would dare brave the furies that awaited it on high.

Meanwhile, I made daily, apprehensive phone calls to Joe's

host, a dear friend who understood my dilemma and also the pup's one boo-boo as a guest: one chewed tennis shoe.

My son, in no time, completely forgot his feathered friends, and any attempt on my part to keep him current with their horrible activities fell on disinterested, or other-interested, ears.

Finally, one night, when I snuck back to my apartment and was met with the usual air attack, I caught them both, loaded them into my Austin without benefit of cage, and drove out into the country, sweeping their tail feathers out of my eyes, until I spied a farm. There I parked until dawn, to be sure that there was other fowl life there, and then turned them loose.

In the pale light I watched them stand indignantly still for a moment till they got their bearings, then raise their voices in the morning chorus, and, with skips, flight, and flutters, they moved into the barnyard, where they were met by a welcome cacophony and where they immediately took command of the situation by sending a dozen white leghorns off in a cloud of fright.

Relieved in the knowledge that they had made themselves at home, and whether welcome by the farmer or not, I knew that they were among their own kind. But the greatest relief of all was the knowledge that I was a man again, for I was never sure, while those roosters were around, that what I *was* sure they believed might not be true—I was just another chicken.

Chapter Nine

But enough of my life with other animals. I had to remember some of them or the book of Joe would not be complete.

I've said it, and so has everyone else since the beginning of time—that every dog has his day. When men say it, they don't for a minute mean real dogs. They hope instead that they, underdogs for the moment, will one day have a day they can call their very own . . . one day of life that will shine like a beacon, lighting the darkened days behind and illuminating those to come.

I am no exception, though I must say that I've had many days of light, of joy, of gratitude for being alive. One of those days that truly lightened the burden of much darkness was the day I met Joe. There has hardly been a day since then that that funny, sweet face of his, those annoying-to-other-people habits of his, haven't brightened my life.

But what about Joe? Has he had his day?

I flatter myself that I've been able to give him many days

of happiness, but if we mean a day of fame, of recognition by that old saying—yes—Joe has had his day, and this is how that day dawned on Joe—and set on me.

Owing to the public nature of my profession and the popular misconception that all actors, tyros or otherwise, are automatically millionaires, most of us, if we're at all aware of our vulnerability, are insured right up to our eyeballs. Perhaps some of us should go even higher and insure against falling hair; toupees are so damned expensive.

The type of insurance I'm talking about is personal liability. At the beginning of my career my wise father had advised me to take some; I did, but only once did it come in handy. Some years ago a dear, sweet, little old cook of ours fell off the back stoop and sued the hell out of me. I'm a pushover for anyone's getting hurt, so when the accident happened I rushed Canary—that was her name, I think, or was it Birdie?—to the semi-fashionable doctor who took care of my fortunately few personal ills, and had him set her arm, which was slightly fractured by the fall. Two weeks afterward I found the meticulously neat bandage he had bound her with removed and the still-swollen arm uncarefully wrapped in tattletale-gray cloth strips, probably ripped from some of my old shirts. I questioned the wisdom of this move, but Chickie, or whatever her name was, repaid me for my concern with a half-hour description of how her dear old grandmother would have handled the situation. There's no use arguing with the prescription of anyone's grandmother, so I forgot the matter.

Then suddenly, one day, while our feathered friend still fluttered happily about the household, I was informed of a suit she was bringing against me for $750, because, according to her doctor, she would never be able to use that arm as she had before the fall off the back stoop.

The dusty ledges and corners of our house seemed to me to be ample evidence that her arm had been nearly useless long before the accident, but apparently that kind of thinking carried little weight with her lawyer, and so, one: my insurance company had to pay off; two: the old crow got fired, or to put it more kindly, left by mutual consent, and three: I took out more personal liability insurance.

That happened early in my acting career, when I was little known. So as my face became increasingly familiar to devotees of the silver screen and I became uneasily aware of my recognizability by strangers, I felt that whatever financial affluence I might or might not be coming into had best be protected from gleaners of the personality field by more and more personal liability.

It wasn't expensive insurance. I'd learned the hard way! So I took out the maximum I thought anyone might sue me for and went on paying it year after year, forgetfully safe in the knowledge that guests or even relatives could slip and slide around my property and, except for my personal concern for their hurts, my assets would remain untampered with even if theirs got bruised.

Then one day, the whole protective process paid off. Joe

and I had departed the small garage-apartment-chicken-yard and moved back to the canyon, which had an un-segregated population of middle- to low-income families. At the same time it retained an all over semi-bohemian atmosphere. Years ago it had been the refuge of downtown folks who wanted a vacation hideaway from the flat heat of the near coastal plains, where Los Angeles had originally settled. It was still studded in my day with assorted shacks, some of which housed struggling young couples inadequately, while others were the luxurious, bachelor residences of somewhat eccentric, single persons of both sexes. Lady artists, lonely tradesmen, and that fast-disappearing race of Jack-of-all-trades-masters-of-none, who can be coaxed into community service for the minor repair jobs that so aggravate the pocketbook, if one is forced to call in a union laborer. . . . Anyway we all loved living in that canyon.

One of these persons was an extravagantly eccentric old lush whose determined means of transportation, much to everyone's consternation because of the traffic, remained the bicycle. He was quite famous in our canyon, not only for his appearance, which was bushy-white-haired and vociferously virile for a man of his age and for the volubility of his wine-soaked tongue, but for a rather extraordinary feat he had achieved a few years before, in celebration of his sixtieth birthday—cycling to San Francisco non-stop. My thoughts on his achievement had always been that no matter how you got to San Francisco it was worth it, but, since I really never had a hankering for the two-wheeled vehicles, motorized or humanized, I simply acknowledged his prowess and tried to avoid being run down by him as I was trimming the curb-line foliage in front of my house.

He was really a ferociously forceful menace as he plummeted down the gentle grade of the canyon, though actually worse than the possibility of being hit by him was the probability that he would stop and chat. His chats were long-winded, one-sided gushers about nothing in particular, but on everything that was wrong with what you were doing at the moment he caught you and how you were doing it. It didn't matter whether you were emptying the garbage, burning leaves, or just idly scratching your head in the sunlight. He always had a better way of doing it, and much more hair to scratch.

By profession he was, a plasterer, but his equally professional avocations included all the other chores that you, as a layman, are so inadequately equipped to perform, at least according to him. But basically he seemed one of those happy few who worked for whatever living he needed, mostly wine, judging from the fruitiness of his breath, no matter what the work happened to be. Twice I had been hornswoggled by him into letting him do my few jealously treasured household chores, and I must say that he did them as adequately, if not as silently, as I did. Garbage-emptying does not require much finesse, but his leaf-burning, while not any more brilliantly successful than mine, did take longer, and since I love the smell of burning leaves the extra dollar or two were worth it, and why not share the wealth.

It was during one of those deliciously idle hours, when you feel that you owe it to yourself to stand by and watch somebody else work, that it dawned on him that I was an actor, and the jerk of recognition his mop-haired head gave when I told him that I was under contract to a movie studio should have been a warning of some kind, I guess, but I was a little flattered by it since I was still in that period of going up in my profession. Television had not yet come along sufficiently to make any actor's face a household appliance, to be used like a magic mirror wired to talk back to you when addressed by anyone with that say-your-face-is-familiar look in his eyes.

The one thing that startled recognition did teach me, however, was that his moments of usefulness to me were over. I didn't think that his fee would increase, but I was sure that his conversation would, and since I was already paying him a good share of his small salary for conversation, I figured that I couldn't afford all of it for gab, either financially or in the interests of freedom from boredom. Still, he never failed to slow down as he saw me in the front garden, but I invented an urgent call from "inside" that produced a masterpiece of hail and farewell as I waved and fled into the house before he could stop. I got into the habit of looking up and down the canyon for a sight of him before I started in earnest on any front-yard activities.

The old boy had another nasty habit besides wine and talk, and whether it originated with him or not I don't know. He acted as a sort of amateur Pied Piper for all the dogs in the neighborhood. His progress down the canyon was often followed by six or eight mutts yapping at his heels. Like an ocean liner leaving port, they acted as an escort to get him out of the neighborhood and into the sea of life beyond. They didn't really bother him, since they all knew him too well to want to do him any harm; they just wanted to get him out of there. He in turn would kick at them and hurl ungentlemanly invectives at them about their ancestry. The noisy procession had usually dwindled to one or two dogs by the time he passed my house, but one day the full pack kept after him all the way down, and Joe, who unlike most dogs really wasn't too disturbed by foreigners on our property, secure, as he had grown to be, that my home was his castle, couldn't resist the impulse to join the carolers. He dashed through his door and out onto the street for the sheer joy of raising his voice

in song with the others, and, careful as he usually is about crossing streets, he mistimed his blind flight into the yipping chorus, and the plasterer, a little more plastered than usual, ran full force into Joe. Over the handle bars he went and onto the street, as Joe, his rib cage badly damaged, took to the hills in screaming agony.

I was at work when this happened, but on coming home I was greeted with the gory details by Will, who worked for me, and by my unpaying tenants, the artist Howard Warshaw and his wife, who lived at that time in the upstairs studio. Joe had finally limped down from the hills and had been packed off to the vet's, suffering from internal injuries that fortunately were not fatal. The plasterer, while somewhat shook up and foul-mouthed angry, had pedaled off down the canyon, apparently indestructible.

I inquired from the three witnesses whether he had been badly hurt, they assured me that he wasn't, and I then drove off to see Joe at the vet's.

If there's anything sadder to behold than a hurt animal, I don't know what it is. Joe had been bound with tape for support and lay in a dejected heap on the floor of his cage. My voice, assuring him that he would be all right, brought only a feeble flick from the very end of his tail, but the doctor promised me that he would be home in two weeks, so back I went—back to a Joe-less house.

When he came home he played the part of the invalid for a day or so, allowing me to shower small attentions on him, then suddenly the third day he decided that he'd had enough and was back once again on his routine of visiting each tree in the neighborhood and waddling miles up and down the canyon in search of new scents and any free female whose charms would be wafted back to him in the right season.

Some months passed for Joe and me, happily baching it, happily on the prowl for companionship, but equally happy, when the day was over, to be a man and his dog.

Then one day a very nice man called at the house, identifying himself by a card as being from my insurance company and, after a few pleasantries, asked if he might meet Joe. For once Joe was in the house and the introduction was consummated with equal dignity from both parties. Joe lent a paw to be shook by the man's proffered hand and proceeded to make a yawning obeisance before him and then rubbed the whole length of his body against his blue-serge trouser leg, leaving the usual deposit of long, multicolored hairs.

"He doesn't look so fierce," said the man in a surprised voice, but the surprise in his voice was nothing compared to the surprise in my face. I broke into an almost uncontrollable guffaw at the thought of Joe's being fierce, but control came when I remembered that he was an insurance man.

"What has Joe done?" I asked, still giggling.

"He attacked a man who lives up the street," he answered soberly.

I said that it was impossible, but the man wasn't laughing, and then he told me the breath-taking story that I was being sued for thirteen thousand dollars and the suer turned out to be my plasterer, whose collarbone had been broken, or so he claimed, in his collision with Joe those many weeks before.

I then related the whole story as it had been told to me by Will, who had since left me to become a rich widow's chauffeur, and by Howard Warshaw, who had also left to teach art at Iowa University. I told him about the other dogs who always chased the old man and asked why he had picked me to sue. The answer was, of course, an at-random eeny-meeny-miney-actor count-down of the people on the street. The fact that his lawyer probably knew that I was insured up to the hilt also had much to do with it. But nothing I told the insurance man impressed him as much as Joe's character. He was smitten with Joe's gentleness, and I think his company would simply have paid the old man off if their representative hadn't met my boy Joe.

He asked me, apologetically, if I would mind testifying in court as to Joe's character, and since I felt partly responsible for the shaping of that sterling character, I accepted gladly.

What it actually meant was backing up my insurance company, who had offered to settle with the injured party to the extent of his injuries. They had offered him $500 to cover his medical expenses, which actually didn't amount to anywhere near that, plus another $500 to compensate him for his loss of work. I questioned the niggardliness of the amount, but from the research they had done on the case they were satisfied that this was more than enough and of course what made them mad, and me too, was the arbitrary sum he demanded of $13,000. Actually he had been unable to work for about two months, and his doctor's bills had been about $200 at the most, and since he had probably never earned more than $150 a month in his life, they felt that $1000 was more than generous.

Since it was no skin off mine, I felt that they could have been a little more generous, but then I found out that they were far from sure that the collision with Joe had been the cause of the broken collarbone, and, furthermore, they questioned the motives of the lawyer and doctor involved. With these assurances from a most reputable insurance company,

I decided to go on their side to try to keep them from being taken.

I guess that I'm the most average kind of American in many respects. I hadn't had much to do with the law or law courts or legal procedures of any kind until I got a divorce, and if anything could turn a law-abiding citizen into a hardened criminal, divorce proceedings in California would go a long way toward it.

In committing myself to defending Joe's character, it had never occurred to me that the insurance company had to take the whole matter into court. I had mentally prepared a statement to the effect that Joe was an impeccably well-mannered dog whose beauty was spiritual rather than physical, though in my eyes he was the best of every breed, belonging to none. I was ready to pledge allegiance to Joe with my hand on my heart, whence that allegiance sprang. Furthermore, I had no mental reservations about his qualifications for star billing in dogdom. Just for whom I was preparing these statements I had no idea, so when I was instructed to appear at the County Courthouse on a certain Tuesday at nine o'clock in the morning, my heart did a slight nip up. When I read the instructions further and discovered that possibly three or four days might be required to try the case—TRY THE CASE—I nearly fainted. Joe was to be put ON TRIAL, a term that frightens me to death even when I read about its happening to someone else . . . and I was to be the Star Witness in defense of Joe's honor.

If ever a man's declaration of devotion to his proverbial best friend was up for examination by the Heavenly Bureau of Internal Revenue, this was it. A panicky moment of wanting to be shed of the whole affair was momentarily quelled by a view of Joe out the window, hogging it in a freshly manured patch of lawn. It was sort of a joyous act of contrition, almost biblical, this habit of his of rolling on his back in the nearest available heap of offal, and whether he meant to purge his soul, Job-like by his abjection in the dust, the sight of it always cheered my heart and carried me back to those wonderful moments in childhood when you were free to let mud ooze through your toes and fashion a feast from it with your hands. I had learned long ago that dust I am and happy I would be to return to it someday . . . I love the earth, and I made up my mind then and there, I loved Joe and would defend his honor, even in the courts of law.

My state of mind the night before the trial started could not have been more complex if I had been going on trial for my own life. I had a dozen mad dreams involving the law—myself behind bars for perjury because Joe had bitten the judge; Joe behind bars with a ball and chain on his tail because of the deep deceit in his nature, discovered by the jury as he wagged his tail while growling viciously at the plaintiff; Joe being thrown out of the courtroom because they couldn't get him to put his right paw on the Bible; me being led off to a cell on a charge of assault with intent to kill, when the plaintiff's lawyer tried to blacken Joe's character; Will, my former houseman, who had been summoned as a witness, dropping dead as a bolt of lightning struck him when he said that Joe was the most savage dog he'd ever seen; Howard Warshaw, whom the insurance company had flown out from Iowa and was comfortably asleep in the guest room, appeared in my dreams as another Michelangelo, painting the walls and ceiling of the city hall with scenes from the creation of the first dog to the final judgment of all dogs on the last day. I was having a hard time locating Joe in the multitude of dog saints when I awoke to the alarm, set early for this very purpose—to break my dreams and to get me up and about the business of this day of days.

I awakened Howard and went into the kitchen to make coffee. I was so concentrating on my own nightmare of this ordeal I was about to go through, I completely forgot that Joe had to go to court too. My reflexes dulled, I automatically unlocked the door and let him out.

Joe's habit on being let out was to head for the front garden, where he proceeded to give the camellias and azaleas their needed shot of acid. As luck would have it, he was doing just this when my dream-addled brain snapped back to reality and I realized that he had to be brought back and collared to go with us. Just as he had finished his last duty as keeper of the camellias, I dashed out and caught him by the stationary leg and hauled him up in my arms and back into the house. I then bolted all doors and accepted his cold look of disdain, without my usual sense of guilt at having interrupted nature and his daily routine.

The main reason for getting up this early was to make it downtown, where the Courthouse was located, to give Joe a ten-time-around-the-block chance to void himself of any possibility of contempt of court by design or necessity. Luckily Howard and I had determined on this precaution the night before. If we had gone straight to court, heaven knows what indignities might have been heaped on officialdom and irreparable damage done to its views of Joe's upbringing.

I dressed carefully and thoughtfully for the occasion, not wanting to appear actorish. I had determinedly avoided mentioning anything about the case to the studio publicity department. I wanted to give the insurance company every chance to win, and publicity might have backfired sympathy against them, but mostly I felt that it was too sacred a trust, this question of Joe's honor, to entrust it to those scavengers of Hollywood inconsequentia. In the same line of thinking I chose a dull gray suit with unpadded shoulders, a plain black tie, black socks, and shined, but not too shined, black shoes. Howard I persuaded, with some difficulty, to forgo his customary artist's disarray, to shave, and to wear a tie. Joe, who is by half his nature fastidiously neat, I didn't even have to brush. He would have to stand or fall on his natural charms and his most unnatural appearance.

The cast was complete except for Will, who would get there on his own recognizance. So we started off happily on the premise, I suppose, that since every dog must have his day this was to be Joe's. We hadn't gone two miles before

Joe decided to feel car sick. I say decided, because I am convinced that dogs do this—decide to be sick, decide to go out, decide every action of their lives. All this nonsense about animal instinct! It's just not possible that their instincts can so perfectly coincide with human inopportunities. Has any dog ever decided that he has to be let out when you were near the door? No, he waits until you're comfortably seated or, preferably, in bed. Has any dog ever been sick in a car when you were driving him off for a pleasure trip? No, only when you are in a hurry and out of the goodness of your heart have taken him along, or on the way to the vet's, or to be washed—anywhere he doesn't like to go.

Joe sensed the drama of this moment, and it made him sick. First he managed that awful sickly grin then he was awfully sick.

Dog lovers, or at moments like this, dog owners, know how to deal with these situations. So it was dealt with. I had a sense of relief in the knowledge that he had decided to do it now and not later, and we were, a little less merrily, on our way again—to court.

Chapter Ten

Downtown Los Angeles is a part of that great, growing city that is assiduously avoided by all its citizens except those who are unfortunate enough to work there. It really isn't any uglier than most downtowns in most American cities, just deader. Someone once said that the reason it's where it is is that they ran out of railroad ties, so the earlier pioneers built it there instead of where it should be, on the coast. Except for official duties, mostly horrid, like getting passports, being examined by state Income Tax reviewers, incorporating, and the like, no one would be caught dead down there. And of course in all cities that's always where the courthouse is—where you wouldn't be caught dead. But one thing we have to admit is that this courthouse is an imposing structure—the more imposing, the less it imposes its functions on you. I had to confess that morning, as it came into towering view, that I had lucidly been spared its embrace during my brief tenancy of the city. This time, however, it looked as if it were going to give me the full, famous treatment.

After Joe had been walked around and around several blocks, mostly through the nearby Japanese section then being rehabilitated after World War II, we slipped inconspicuously into the great open maw of the Court Building, with its glaring stone-engraved mottoes of what the Law can do for the people or what it will do to them if they step on its toes. We stood patiently in the great marble corridors waiting for an elevator. Joe loves cool surfaces, so he promptly spread-eagled on the floor to take the full benefit of its cold comfort on his belly. Several sensitive souls remarked on his beauty or, as they called it, cuteness, and he graciously allowed several pats on the head and ungraciously yipped as someone trod on his tail. Then the stainless-steel door of the elevator opened and we stepped in. The operator took one look at Joe and said in well-rehearsed, clipped, official language: "Expected in court?" to which I answered unreasonably: "Of course," and we were on our way to the nineteenth floor.

A lower-ceilinged marble replica of the corridor on the ground floor greeted us above, and we walked down the empty hall with Joe's nails beating a sharp tattoo ahead of us. He seemed almost eager now, and as we got to the frosted-glass door of the courtroom, he made a final hind-end-up gesture of prayer, shook himself, and we entered.

The interior was clinically legal. Mahogany-finished rails separated the spectators, who were nonexistent as yet, from the court of action, also deserted when we arrived except for a well-cast, burly policeman who ushered us unceremoniously into the spectator section. Howard and I sat tenuously on the legal chairs, and Joe resigned himself to his fate, at out feet.

First to bring us his encouraging company was the lawyer for the insurance company. He shook hands with me, gave Howard a reserved and questioning look, and patted Joe on the head, murmuring what seemed to me a very unlegal but hopeful: "Nice doggy." Howard later claimed that he said, "Nice dog," but I swear that it was "Nice doggy." He then proceeded to tell us in a hushed and husky voice that no one could overhear because no one was there but us culprits, the policeman having left just before we came in, that we were not to worry about today's session because most of the day would be taken up choosing a jury. A JURY!

I'd dreamed about a jury the night before, but it never occurred to me that this insignificant little case would require the opinions of twelve good men and true women. My look must have told him this, for he explained in even more hushed tones that $13,000 was not a small case.

Of course I had been blithely going on the assumption that the real import of all this was the defamation of Joe's character. I had prepared so well for the part of defender of my faith in him that I'd completely forgotten the $13,000. If it had been my $13,000, things would have been different, I'm sure. Then it would have been: to hell with his honor and what was that stupid mutt doing running out in the street and getting himself hit and someone else hurt?

But things came quickly back into their proper perspective. My role as the male Portia whittled itself down to a Bassanio, and when the lawyer left us to draw up his brief or something, Howard and I were suddenly ravaged by a terrible case of hard-to-suppress giggles. In this drama we were definitely miscast—by ourselves.

By the time we regained partial control, people suddenly began to swarm into the room. Some were formidably official-looking, others looked as out of place as the two of us. Only Joe retained an individuality, by being the only dog in the room—thank God.

Things began to happen in a definite pattern; people came and went as if they were meant to. Nobody spoke to us at all. Little groups of two or three gathered together, but though our ears were straining to understand something, anything of the meaning of all this, their voices were too low, and the few words we did catch flew over our comprehension like legal eagles. As far as we were concerned the arm of the law was too long even to shake its hand.

Individuals from the small multitude were conducted into what we gathered was the jury box, and then for the first time we began to understand what was happening. They were going to select the jury. First, the plaintiff-plasterer was shown to the group. He was a pathetic, sober old man, all his bicycle braggadocio gone out of him now. Then I was asked to step out and make myself known as the defendant and then retired once again behind the line of scrimmage, next to Howard, on the bench. Joe was then paraded out and, once identified as the culprit, yawned his great yawn and came back to join us.

One by one the prospective jury members were asked three questions each: Are you prejudiced against dogs? Are you prejudiced against men who ride bicycles? Are you prejudiced against actors? Prejudiced against actors, indeed! What a humiliating question! But then I remembered the wonderful fact that the Number One country club in our community has a rule—No Jews or Actors Allowed—and I felt much better. . . . I like minority groups.

Howard, upon hearing this last insulting question, nodded strongly in agreement. I gave him a swift, hard kick that caught Joe a glancing blow, and he made his presence felt once again with a pathetic little yelp. The entire cast, for so they had become to me in this now inescapable little drama, turned a Rockette-timed look in our direction. From the bemused expressions on all faces, except the plaintiff's lawyer, whom we had now identified by his unrelieved expression of gloom, I could tell that we were in the company of some dog tolerators, at least, and probably a few dog lovers.

Several jurymen were questioned and accepted and another had just been questioned and had answered negatively to all three, when suddenly my lawyer (I now claimed him as mine) jumped to his feet and hurled a further question at him.

"Sir, I believe you are a mailman by profession?"

"Yes, sir."

"Do you mean to tell me you have no prejudices against dogs?"

My ears pricked up; this boy knew his business. He wasn't going to have any dog-prejudiced mailman on our route—I mean jury.

But the mailman stuck to his guns and maintained his devotion to our animal friends in spite of his admitting to several near encounters with their teeth, an admission that came out under still further, not-too-cross examination. My lawyer had made his point. The simple three questions were not going to satisfy him, but now he could afford to be gentle and he soothed the mailman's ruffled nerves and accepted him.

About eight jurors made it and were in the box when the ninth appeared. She was a matronly woman in middle years with a sweet face. I was rooting for her; she had to like dogs—and possibly even actors.

She passed the standard test, and I thought that she was in, when once again my man lashed out: "Madam," (she could never have been one) "do you feel that actors are more susceptible to lawsuits than other people?"

What was he getting at? He might lose our chance to have this lovely lady, possibly from Pasadena, on our side.

She drew herself up to a pouty, five foot two and very calmly and concisely delivered herself one of the sweetest sentiments I have ever heard about my battered profession.

"I most certainly do! I think it is wicked the way people take advantage of actors just because they are in the public eye. They're just the same as other people, but everything they do the press publicizes. Why, the poor dears don't have a chance to have a private life. Accidents happen to everyone, but nobody pays any attention to them, but if an actor is involved in one, it's a headline. I think it's dreadful the way people sue them for the slightest thing."

On and on she went, and of course out and out went her chances of being on the jury. But she was telling the other jury members more by her warm indignation than Clarence Darrow could ever have done with the utmost oratory.

We may have lost one sympathetic member, but maybe we had gained eight, for I could read agreement with her sentiments on all those other blatantly poker faces.

There were no more dramatic incidents in the selection of the other four, but it had taken all morning. We were dismissed for the rest of the day and told to come back tomorrow at the same time.

Our routine remained the same the next morning, getting up early, keeping Joe inside till departure time, driving slowly downtown so he wouldn't get sick, the long, last walk around the courthouse for dehydration purposes, and then into the jaws of justice once again.

All the jury members had been duly selected, and now we were set for the trial to begin.

The case was stated by the plasterer's lawyer, and it did

sound as if the poor fellow had been in a dreadful plight. Out of work because of the broken collarbone, he had lain in his humble shack, racked with pain. I was almost wishing that I had refused to defend Joe's honor, had let the insurance company pay out the $13,000, and was rid of the whole mess, when Joe suddenly discovered a flea, or I prefer to think it was just an itch, and thumped out a long tattoo on the floor of the courtroom. The jury's attention was diverted for a moment, a restless but welcome giggle spread over the room, and the lawyer had a hard time getting them back under his spell. I quelled Joe's itch with a prolonged scratching of the irritating area and resolved to pull myself together and, come what may, defend this lovely dog with all my heart and soul.

A map was shown to establish where and how the accident had taken place, and then the lawyer called his first witness, the doctor who had set the collarbone.

The injury was described, and we were told how painful it was and how long it took to mend. A doctor's tale was told in the usual unintelligible, medical terms, and so the lawyer brought some X-rays into evidence. A viewing apparatus was set up, plugged in, and there for all of us to see were the broken bones.

At this point Joe decided to sit up in his best food-begging manner, and that did it. The idea of a dog sitting up at the sight of the X-rayed bones, though of course it wasn't the bones at all, simply his genius for dramatic timing, undid the courtroom and even the judge couldn't keep a straight face.

The whole episode was so charming, everyone enjoyed it, and order was restored to the court automatically by the sense of relief they all felt.

Only two people obviously remained unsmiling and looked as though they wished with all their hearts that Joe had not been brought to the trial . . . in fact they wished that he was dead.

During the next two days Joe brought lightness several times to the procedure with his barks and one great yawn accompanied by a loud dog-yawn sound during a particularly dull passage. Most of the time he played it smooth and quiet.

Howard was called as a witness, giving brilliant, eyewitness testimony that it was only secondarily Joe's fault since the plasterer struck Joe and Joe did not attack him.

Will gave the most beautiful tribute to his character with words I'll never forget. "He may not be the purtiest dog in the world, but he's the kindest one I've ever met."

The insurance lawyer was brilliant in pointing out that there was no definite proof of the broken collarbone being caused by the collision with Joe. He played up the fact that actors were the innocent victims of all sorts of chicanery, to the point where my appearance on the witness stand was utterly anticlimactic. In the eyes of the jury I was already one of the most poignant cases of victimization ever known. All I did was to back up Will's magnificent statement of Joe's character, though with nowhere near as effective a characterization. Without a doubt I was the dullest member of the cast.

At no time during the trial did any press come into the room, even out of routine courtesy, as I understand they always do. I was delighted, as I really wanted Joe's case to stand on its own—and it did.

The jury brought in the verdict of NOT GUILTY—the insurance company was absolved of all risk and the poor plasterer didn't even get the thousand he would have gotten had he accepted their offer and not held out in the hope of twelve thousand more.

The case was dismissed, followed by much celebration and congratulations by officials, lawyers, and jury members. Joe received dozens of pats and many ridiculous compliments and pleasantries with resigned complacency. He shook himself, dislodging great clouds of fur as if to be done with the whole, dull experience . . . and then the press arrived.

An early-departing juror had told the story downstairs, and the press was on us like flies. Here was a story. "Actor Defends Dog's Honor in Court."

Pictures of Joe went out on the wire services. Joe and I were posed in loving poses and the picture was in every paper. Long columns appeared, telling the whole story, and we became a one-day wonder that everyone thoroughly enjoyed.

There was a small party in the canyon that night, and through it all Joe slept in front of the fire—hero for a day, but it was night now and time to sleep.

Three days later, after dozens of telegrams and phone calls from friends and family around the country, I was devoutly glad that the whole incident apparently was over. Joe was vindicated; that's all I really wanted. I had to recognize the fact that it did make a good story, and any actor who isn't grateful for good publicity is a liar . . . but I'd had it, and so the sooner Joe and I became just another man and his dog, the better.

But as I started this chapter, so it must end. There are

many misconceptions about my profession, owing to its public nature, and one is that an actor can ever lead a quiet life.

The mailbox suddenly was stuffed with letters, fan letters . . . all addressed to Joe!

I reprint one to give you an idea of what the human mind can stoop to in order to get into the act:

Mr. Joe Price
c/o Actor Vincent Price
Hollywood, California

Dearest precious, pretty, pretty, Joesie, Woesie,

My name is Millie. I'm a Cocker Spaniel—at least part of me is. The rest I'd rather not tell you about. (Perhaps you'd care to find out for yourself) but I'm an animal . . . and I'm a GIRL.

My Mommie read me the story about you and your Daddie. He must be a nice man, and I'll go see all his pictures now that I know he loves good, little dogs like you, Joe.

I'd love to meet you some night when the moon is full—dog! Could we ever yowl!

Drop me a card, Joe dear, and I'm all yours!

Bow Wow until whenever,
Millie

This was one of the best and gives you an idea of the level of their messages. I use it because it's the only one that even gives me a mention!

A few were rather touching; some were just downright disgusting, and one I wouldn't even dare to read aloud in front of my sporty friends.

Fortunately Joe's fan mail petered out rapidly, and while I was tempted to answer some of the fruitier ones, in Joe's name of course, I resisted it and found myself, a week after the trial, finally back to normal.

I was sitting that night happily having a drink on my front patio when a knock came on the gate. Joe came out with the short series of barks he uses to try to prove that he's a watchdog, and I went out to see who it was.

I opened the gate part way and came face to face with a handsome, well-dressed couple. The lady's eyes were riveted on the ground. She addressed it with baited breath: "Was that Joe?"

I allowed as how it was, but that he'd gone inside. Then she lifted her big (I thought doglike) eyes to mine and said:

"Are you Joe's daddy?"

This stumped me, but I guessed that I might as well say yes. She wanted me to be, obviously.

Then the man said that they would like to talk to me about something very important, and I let them in hoping that they wouldn't make further fools of themselves and that I could control my temper if they did.

They were obviously an earnest couple, and I felt that I might have been wrong about the lady's opening remarks about my relationship to Joe.

They undid a copious brief case and laid out some papers for my inspection. I couldn't miss seeing the large print heading the first sheet. "VINCENT PRICE FOR MAYOR OF BEVERLY HILLS."

I have a habit at times of complete surprise and confusion, of letting out a grunt that apparently sounds to other people as if I wanted them to repeat what they've said.

And they repeated it. A long story about how I would make the ideal mayor of Beverly Hills on the anti-vivisection ticket. How the story of Joe and me would capture the hearts of all true animal lovers, and where were there more true animal lovers than in Beverly Hills? I felt as if I were drowning in their words. This could not be happening. I spluttered and puffed, trying to stop the torrent, and just as I was about to go down for the third time and the picture of myself at the mayor's desk in the Beverly Hills City Hall was swimming before my eyes, I came to my senses and announced with finality that I thought it a most flattering offer, but I was not a resident of that fair city, living as I did across the city line, and therefore could not accept the nomination. With equal finality they accepted this fact, made short farewells to me, looked longingly around for a glimpse of Joe, and left.

I was a private citizen once again.

As I settled back to enjoy the twilight's cool beauty, and

Joe, assured by the sound of the gate that they had gone, came out to join me in my reverie, visions of my narrow escape from political power conjured up some pretty ridiculous pictures. . . .

Joe and I were riding through the streets of Beverly Hills, ticker tape curling from the windows above, signs and banners lined the curb, and a mixed chorus of a thousand voices swelled into the sky declaring Joe's daddy as the perfect mayor. Joe's daddy indeed!

Well, come to think of it, why not? If the shoe fits why not wear it? After all, it's a wise child who knows . . . and vice versa!

Postscript

Thus endeth the book of Joe.

The trial was the highlight of Joe's life, though he played it with the utmost nonchalance. It was certainly one of the moments I'll always remember, for no matter how ridiculous it all seems now, those last two people were dead serious, and I suppose that a dog *can* help win an election. It's been done before.

At this moment in my life the list of livestock, while slightly less varied than the Ark's, is almost as numerous: twelve freewheeling pigeons; ten caged pigeons of various breeds and feather; seventeen land turtles, brought by loving friends to keep one company that wandered in off the streets and range in size from a large beach stone to a small pancake; fourteen goldfish, seven rescued from a plastic bubble in which they swam around a clown's head in a circus picture I made two years ago, and seven others purchased or won at greater expense at country fairs by Mary's prowess at pitching Ping-pong balls into minute goldfish bowls; and three dogs, Prudence, now a slightly elderly lady hockey player with an infectious coyness, Pasquale, who is the most endearing coward ever to threaten a milkman with his ferocious bark from a more-than-safe distance, and Joe.

Joe has developed a deep yowl that accompanies every increasing complaint against the human race. He is hard to please, but then so much love has been showered on him by me, I guess he figures that he might as well wring my emotions dry. In his spry old age he's become a bit of a bore, conveniently deaf, insistently demanding to get his way, but he's mine (all mine, according to Mary) and I still love him.

I have said much about Joe's physical attributes . . . his looks, which to my love-blind eyes are the way a dog should look. They are singular, and were from the beginning. Age has lent him little distinction. He has, in fact, changed in only one way since he reached maturity—he has gotten broader owing to laziness and the fact that we're afraid to give him the run of the canyon since the traffic doubles daily, it seems, here in Los Angeles.

Mary pointed out the other day that he had indeed become a fur-upholstered coffee table, and I had to add, *sotto voce,* with Duncan Phyfe legs. You can't quite serve high tea for three on his back, but pretty near. Besides, he wouldn't hold still for such an indignity. But the idea of training him to carry a couple of beers does have some appeal. However, I must remember . . . "You can't teach an old dog new tricks," and Joe's been an old dog for some time, now . . . almost from the beginning.

Dogs have come and gone and may continue to come and go in my life. Though I have loved them all dearly, delighted in their devotion, devoted myself to them, there will never be another Joe. Something about him—banal, commonplace, but never mediocre—intrigues me. If I were a dog, I'd want to be Joe. And I feel sincerely that, while I'm sure he has enough sense not to want to be human (being the most content-to-be-a-dog dog I've ever known), should it ever cross his mind, he might want to be like me. We have rapport. We can love or be loved without drowning in bathos. He attaches importance to my love for him when he needs to feel important, and his love for me is an important, if understated up till now, part of my life. I love him with a love I seemed to lose with my lost youth, to misquote Mrs. Browning.

In Joe I sense the gentle conquest of man over nature and of nature's reciprocal kindness to man. I see in him the possibility of the Peaceable Kingdom.

There is something divine in the plan of man and animal being together. Man is an animal of course, but our diviner power of communication may get us no closer to the heavenly crown than the voiceless devotion of our lower-ordered friends. We may, in fact, be talking ourselves out of simplicity, out of trust, out of love . . . out of humanity.

There's an old song hit, "Happiness Is Just a Thing Called

Joe." I'll sing it long and loud, and when the book of Joe is closed, I know I'll have that hurting in my heart and mind, and that Hamlet—oh, that ever-quotable Hamlet—will be able to express it better than I can: "Take him for all in all, I shall not look upon his like again."

The Fund for Animals

Vincent Price with Cleveland and Martha Amory and their beloved Siberian Huskies, Ivan and Peter

From the personal collection of Victoria Price.

Cleveland and Martha Amory were two of my parents' dearest friends, as well as lifelong dog lovers and animal rights advocates. They were also my godparents. It is with great pleasure that the Vincent Price Family Legacy is donating a portion of the proceeds from *The Book of Joe* to the Fund for Animals, the extraordinary animal rights organization founded by Cleveland Amory. It is our hope that sales of *The Book of Joe* will not only benefit the animals we love, but also raise awareness of what we can all do to advocate on their behalf.

—Victoria Price

The Fund for Animals

Founded by author and social critic Cleveland Amory in 1967, the Fund for Animals provides hands-on direct care through the nation's largest and most diverse network of animal sanctuaries and wildlife rehabilitation centers. At these animal care centers, in California, Massachusetts, Oregon, and Texas, dedicated staff and volunteers provide for thousands of injured, orphaned, and mistreated animals in need each year, giving dozens of species, including horses, chimpanzees, birds, bobcats, rabbits, and others, a second chance. The Fund provides veterinary students with valuable training through internship programs, and educates visitors and the public about critical animal protection issues and humane solutions to human-wildlife conflicts. The Fund for Animals carries on Cleveland Amory's historic legacy of protecting animals through advocacy campaigns and public policy strategy, especially in protecting wild animals from inhumane and unsporting methods of cruelty.

About the Author

Vincent Price (1911–1993) was a prolific American actor, best known for his roles in horror films such as *House of Wax*, *The Mad Magician*, and *The Fly*. He also starred in a series of Edgar Allan Poe film adaptations directed by Roger Corman, including *The Pit and the Pendulum*, *The Raven*, and *The Masque of the Red Death*. Originally from St. Louis, Missouri, and educated at Yale University, Price began his acting career while pursuing a master of fine arts at the University of London. His vast work included more than one hundred roles in film, radio, and television, with his singular, deep voice becoming synonymous with PBS's *Mystery!* and BBC Radio's *The Price of Fear*. An avid art collector, Price and his wife, Mary Grant, established the Vincent Price Art Museum at East Los Angeles College with two thousand pieces from their own collection. Price is the author of *I Like What I Know: A Visual Autobiography* and *The Book of Joe*.